Reflections of

25 years

of the Borough of

State

College

Government

1996-2023

Thomas Daubert

Published by the Borough of State College

Primary Author Borough Historian Thomas Daubert

Editor and Co-Author Communications Intern Anna Lumsargis

Advisor and Contributor Communications Specialist Kayla Lafferty

Borough of State College

243 South Allen Street, State College, PA

814-234-7100

Table of Contents

Preface

This monograph is being written primarily to extend the work of Mayor Arnold Addison's book *Issues & Personalities in the First Hundred Years of State College Government*, published in early 1996 as the Borough began its celebration of our Centennial. In addition, the book attempts to build on the government portion of the latest history of State College from *Story of the Century — Borough of State College, PA 1896-1996* by Jo Chesworth, also published in early 1996. This monograph will start with the 1996 Centennial Celebration.

The Addison book consisted of six chapters titled "The Founders of State College", "State College Council Membership", "Local Government Issues", "Elected and Appointed Leaders in Local Government", "Historic Milestones in Local Government", and "Reflections on Local Government Experiences."

Originally, I planned to update the Addison book as he requested me to do in 1999, before his death in 2000. Upon reflection, this is almost impossible, as Arnold's writing style was personal in many ways. Thus, this monograph should stand alone in relating to more recent activities of the Borough.

Listings of Council membership, Burgesses and Mayors, and Managers are included together with comments on these office holders since the mid-1990s. The Authorities, Boards, and Commissions (ABCs), not previously included, are discussed with their major responsibilities added. Borough Citizenship Awards to individuals and organizations are given expanded coverage, with the recipients and their contributions identified. A major portion of the contents is a discussion of the forward-looking legislation and actions of Council since 1996.

~ Thomas Daubert, Borough of State College Historian

Introduction

Activities of the Borough of State College government from 1996 to 2019 are outlined, with important activities and actions identified for each year. The activities for 2020 to 2022 during the COVID-19 pandemic are briefly summarized.

This monograph primarily discusses the major activities, legislative actions, people (elected, staff, and volunteer), and primary accomplishments of the Borough of State College government, starting with the Borough's Centennial Year in 1996. Its predecessor was Arnold Adison's book noted in the Preface, but it differs in that it is focused less on personal experiences and more on the history of what has happened. Although most of this work focuses on the years starting with the Centennial, earlier items not covered in Addison's book are often included where appropriate. Duplications are few but are included when deemed necessary to cover the history of the Borough of State College government more completely.

Major topics are presented in the Preface with brief comments given at the beginning of each section.

Borough of State College

Mission Statement

State College Borough's mission is to enhance the quality of life by fostering a safe, vibrant, diverse, and sustainable community; by providing innovative, cost-effective services; and by allocating resources efficiently with professionalism, integrity, transparency, and accountability.

Core Values

Core values provide the foundation for the Borough of State College. They are the basis of all decisions and actions. These are guiding values that affect the manner in which programs are defined and resources are allocated.

Integrity
Honesty
Innovation
Accountability Value of Staff
Fiscal Responsibility

Author's Note

The persons responsible for this writing and editing are noted below. Many others involved with Borough government have contributed to this publication.

The primary author is Dr. Thomas Daubert, who has been involved in areas of Borough government for the past 40 years. He started as a proponent of the State College neighborhoods and their plans and later as a member of the Planning Commission. He then served for 24 years as an elected six-term member of Borough Council, serving as Council President three times for two-year periods. Upon retirement from Borough Council at the end of 2017, he was appointed and now serves as Borough Historian.

The main assistant in this project is Anna Lumsargis, a 4th-year student at Penn State, who has served as a communications intern during the entire 2024 year. She is majoring in Public Relations with two minors, including Digital Media Trends and Analytics and History. She will receive a BA in Public Relations in May 2025. She has contributed both in content and format, being the major contributor in the formatting and editing of the book.

Kayla Lafferty, the Borough staff Communications Specialist, is the liaison and consultant on the project. She contributed in many ways to gathering material and staff support throughout the project. She holds a BA in Journalism and an MPS in Strategic Communications, both from Penn State.

State College Neighborhoods

State College consists of nine neighborhoods, most of which were defined in the early 1990s, with minor changes and additions made since. The current boundaries are shown on the attached map.

College Heights is the entire area north of the University and is primarily residential.

Holmes Foster is west of South Atherton Street and north of Westerly Parkway. The area is primarily residential, except for the area along West College Avenue.

Highlands is east of South Atherton Street and north of Easterly Parkway, with the Downtown commercial area along the north boundary. This large area includes a large portion of Penn State University student housing as well as fraternities with residential areas throughout, but primarily to the south.

State College South is the triangular area south of Easterly Parkway, east of South Atherton Street, and west of University Drive. The area is primarily residential.

Greentree is the residential area south of Westerly Parkway, as shown on the map.

Orchard Park adjoins Greentree to the south.

Tusseyview is the area southwest of South Atherton Street and is a mix of residential and small commercial.

Vallamont is a small area east of the Highlands and University Drive and is primarily single-family residential.

Nittany Hills East is primarily a single-family residential area between University Drive and the Centre Hills Country Club.

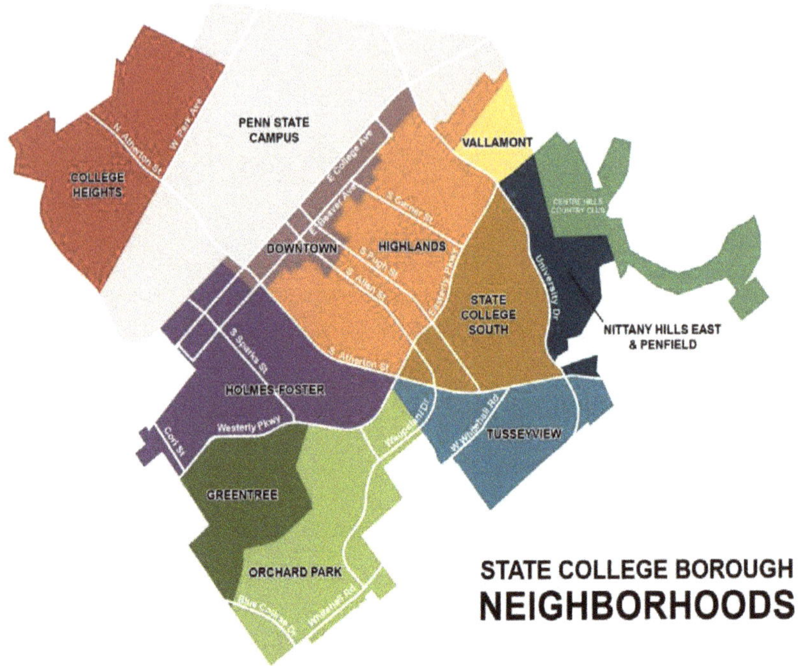

Map of State College neighborhoods courtesy of the Borough of State College.

Council Membership
1996-2023

This section lists the citizens who have served on Borough Council from 1996 to 2023. Councils from 1896 to 1996 are listed in the Addison document.

Council members are elected for four-year terms. Council elections are held every odd year. The seven Council members are elected in two groups — four members and three members in alternate odd years, so that the terms of all members do not expire in the same year. The resignation of any Council member causes the vacancy to be filled by the remaining Council members until the next odd-year election, where the remainder of the term, if any, will be filled by the appropriate four- or two-year term. Council members may only serve for a maximum of two four-year terms in succession. They cannot run for reelection until two years following the required break in service.

This section includes all Council members for each year, as well as the Mayor, the Borough Manager, the Solicitor, and the Assistant Borough Secretary, who interacts with Council, maintains meeting minutes, and signs official paperwork.

1996

Welch, William L., Jr., Mayor .... 01/01/1994 — 12/31/1997

Daubert, Thomas E., President .... 01/01/1992 — 12/31/1999

Hahn, Donald M. .... 01/01/1996 — 12/31/1999

Knauer, Janet K. .... 01/01/1994 — 12/31/1997

Lavin, Ruth K. .... 01/01/1986 — 12/31/1997

McCarl, Richard L. .... 01/01/1996 — 12/31/1999

McManis, Jean W. .... 01/01/1988 — 12/31/1999

Wettstone, Jerry R. .... 01/01/1989 — 12/31/1997

Marshall, Peter S., Manager .... 1986 — Indefinite Term

Davis, Ronald A., Assistant Manager..... 03/29/1988 — Indefinite Term

Natalie, Barbara J., Assistant Secretary .... 1987 — Indefinite Term

Williams, Terry J., Solicitor .... 1987 — Indefinite Term

1997

Welch, William L., Jr., Mayor .... 01/01/1994 — 12/31/1997

Daubert, Thomas E., President .... 01/01/1992 — 12/31/1999

Hahn, Donald M. .... 01/01/1996 — 12/31/1999

Knauer, Janet K. .... 01/01/1994 — 12/31/1997

Lavin, Ruth K. .... 01/01/1986 — 12/31/1997

McCarl, Richard L. .... 01/01/1996 — 12/31/1999

McManis, Jean W. .... 01/01/1988 — 12/31/1999

Wettstone, Jerry R. .... 01/01/1989 — 12/31/1997

Marshall, Peter S., Manager .... 1986 — Indefinite Term

Davis, Ronald A., Assistant Manager..... 03/29/1988 — Indefinite Term

Natalie, Barbara J., Assistant Secretary .... 1987 — Indefinite Term

Williams, Terry J., Solicitor .... 1987 — Indefinite Term

1998

Welch, William L., Jr., Mayor .... 01/01/1994 — 12/31/2001

McManis, Jean W., President .... 01/01/1988 — 12/31/1999

Daubert, Thomas E.. 01/01/1992 — 12/31/1999

Goreham, Elizabeth A...................................... 01/01/1998 — 12/31/2001

Hahn, Donald M. .... 01/01/1996 — 12/31/1999

Knauer, Janet K. .... 01/01/1994 — 12/31/2001

McCarl, Richard L.. 01/01/1996 — 12/31/1999

Meyer, James H. .... 01/01/1998 — 12/31/2001

Marshall, Peter S., Manager .... 1986 — Indefinite Term

Davis, Ronald A., Assistant Manager..... 03/29/1988 — Indefinite Term

Natalie, Barbara J., Assistant Secretary .... 1987 — Indefinite Term

Williams, Terry J., Solicitor .... 1987 — Indefinite Term

Council 1998-1999. First row: Janet Knauer, William Welch (Mayor), Jean McManis (President), Richard McCarl. Second Row: Donald Hahn, Elizabeth Goreham, James Meyer, Thomas Daubert. Photo by the Borough of State College.

1999

Welch, William L., Jr., Mayor .... 01/01/1994 — 12/31/2001
McManis, Jean W., President .... 01/01/1988 — 12/31/1999
Daubert, Thomas E. .... 01/01/1992 — 12/31/1999
Goreham, Elizabeth A. .... 01/01/1998 — 12/31/2001
Hahn, Donald M. .... 01/01/1996 — 12/31/1999
Knauer, Janet K. .... 01/01/1994 — 12/31/2001
McCarl, Richard L. .... 01/01/1996 — 12/31/1999
Meyer, James H. .... 01/01/1998 — 12/31/2001
Marshall, Peter S., Manager .... 1986 — Indefinite Term
Davis, Ronald A., Assistant Manager ..... 03/29/1988 — Indefinite Term
Natalie, Barbara J., Assistant Secretary .... 1987 — Indefinite Term
Williams, Terry J., Solicitor .... 1987 — Indefinite Term

2000

Welch, William L., Jr., Mayor .... 01/01/1994 — 12/31/2001
Knauer, Janet K., President .... 01/01/1994 — 12/31/2001
Daubert, Thomas E. .... 01/01/1992 — 12/31/2003
Dauler, Catherine G. .... 01/01/2000 — 12/31/2003
Goreham, Elizabeth A. .... 01/01/1998 — 12/31/2001
McCarl, Richard L. .... 01/01/1996 — 12/31/2003
McManis, Jean W. .... 01/01/1988 — 12/31/2003
Meyer, James H. .... 01/01/1998 — 12/31/2001
Marshall, Peter S., Manager .... 1986 — Indefinite Term
Davis, Ronald A., Assistant Manager ..... 03/29/1988 — Indefinite Term
Natalie, Barbara J., Assistant Secretary .... 1987 — Indefinite Term
Williams, Terry J., Solicitor .... 1987 — Indefinite Term

2001

Welch, William L., Jr., Mayor .... 01/01/1994 — 12/31/2001

Knauer, Janet K., President .... 01/01/1994 — 12/31/2001

Daubert, Thomas E. .... 01/01/1992 — 12/31/2003

Dauler, Catherine G. .... 01/01/2000 — 12/31/2003

Goreham, Elizabeth A. .... 01/01/1998 — 12/31/2001

McCarl, Richard L. .... 01/01/1996 — 12/31/2003

McManis, Jean W. .... 01/01/1988 — 12/31/2003

Meyer, James H. .... 01/01/1998 — 12/31/2001

Marshall, Peter S., Manager .... 1986 — Indefinite Term

Davis, Ronald A., Assistant Manager ..... 03/29/1988 — Indefinite Term

Natalie, Barbara J., Assistant Secretary .... 1987 — Indefinite Term

Williams, Terry J., Solicitor .... 1987 — Indefinite Term

2002

Welch, William L., Jr., Mayor .... 01/01/1994 — 12/31/2005

McCarl, Richard L, President .... 01/01/1996 — 12/31/2003

Daubert, Thomas E. .... 01/01/1992 — 12/31/2003

Dauler, Catherine G. .... 01/01/2000 — 12/31/2003

Goreham, Elizabeth A. .... 01/01/1998 — 12/31/2005

Knauer, Janet K. .... 01/01/1994 — 12/31/2005

McManis, Jean W. .... 01/01/1988 — 12/31/2003

Meyer, James H. .... 01/01/1998 — 12/31/2005

Marshall, Peter S., Manager .... 1986 — Indefinite Term

Davis, Ronald A., Assistant Manager ..... 03/29/1988 — Indefinite Term

Natalie, Barbara J., Assistant Secretary .... 1987 — Indefinite Term

Williams, Terry J., Solicitor .... 1987 — Indefinite Term

2003

Welch, William L., Jr., Mayor .... 01/01/1994 — 12/31/2005
McCarl, Richard L, President .... 01/01/1996 — 12/31/2003
Daubert, Thomas E. .... 01/01/1992 — 12/31/2003
Dauler, Catherine G. .... 01/01/2000 — 12/31/2003
Goreham, Elizabeth A. .... 01/01/1998 — 12/31/2005
Knauer, Janet K. .... 01/01/1994 — 12/31/2005
McManis, Jean W. .... 01/01/1988 — 12/31/2003
Meyer, James H. .... 01/01/1998 — 12/31/2005
Marshall, Peter S., Manager .... 1986 —Resigned 09/15/2003
Fountaine, Thomas J., II, Manager ....11/05/2003 — Indefinite Term
Davis, Ronald A., Assistant Manager..... 03/29/1988 — Indefinite Term
Natalie, Barbara J., Assistant Secretary .... 1987 — Indefinite Term
Williams, Terry J., Solicitor .... 1987 — Indefinite Term

2004

Welch, William L., Jr., Mayor .... 01/01/1994 — 12/31/2005
Daubert, Thomas E., President .... 01/01/1992 — 12/31/2007
Dauler, Catherine G. .... 01/01/2000 — 12/31/2007
Goreham, Elizabeth A. .... 01/01/1998 — 12/31/2005
Humphrey, Craig R. .... 01/01/2004 — 12/31/2007
Kern, Jeffrey R. .... 01/01/2004 — 12/31/2007
Knauer, Janet K. .... 01/01/1994 — 12/31/2005
Meyer, James H. .... 01/01/1998 — 12/31/2005
Fountaine, Thomas J., II, Manager ....11/05/2003 — Indefinite Term
Davis, Ronald A., Assistant Manager..... 03/29/1988 — Indefinite Term
Natalie, Barbara J., Assistant Secretary .... 1987 — 12/31/2004
Williams, Terry J., Solicitor .... 1987 — Indefinite Term

2005

Welch, William L., Jr., Mayor .... 01/01/1994 — 12/31/2005
Daubert, Thomas E., President .... 01/01/1992 — 12/31/2007
Dauler, Catherine G. .... 01/01/2000 — 12/31/2007
Goreham, Elizabeth A.................................. 01/01/1998 — 12/31/2005
Humphrey, Craig R. .... 01/01/2004 — 12/31/2007
Kern, Jeffrey R... 01/01/2004 — 12/31/2007
McCarl, Richard L. .... 06/06/2004 — 12/31/2005
Meyer, James H. .... 01/01/1998 — 12/31/2005
Fountaine, Thomas J., II, Manager ....11/05/2003 — Indefinite Term
Davis, Ronald A., Assistant Manager..... 03/29/1988 — Indefinite Term
Hanscom, Cynthia S., Assistant Secretary . 04/13/2005 — Indefinite Term
Williams, Terry J., Solicitor .... 1987 — Indefinite Term

2006

Welch, William L., Jr., Mayor .... 01/01/1994 — 12/31/2009
Dauler, Catherine G., President .... 01/01/2000 — 12/31/2007
Daubert, Thomas E.. 01/01/1992 — 12/31/2007
Filippelli, Ronald L. .... 01/01/2006 — 12/31/2009
Goreham, Elizabeth A.................................. 01/01/1998 — 12/31/2009
Hahn, Donald M.. 01/01/2006 — 12/31/2009
Humphrey, Craig R. .... 01/01/2004 — 12/31/2007
Kern, Jeffrey R... 01/01/2004 — 12/31/2007
Fountaine, Thomas J., II, Manager ....11/05/2003 — Indefinite Term
Davis, Ronald A., Assistant Manager........... 03/29/1988 — 08/31/2006
Kurtz, Thomas J., Assistant Manager .. 03/20/2006 — Indefinite Term
Hanscom, Cynthia S., Assistant Secretary . 04/13/2005 — Indefinite Term
Williams, Terry J., Solicitor .... 1987 — Indefinite Term

2007

Welch, William L., Jr., Mayor .... 01/01/1994 — 12/31/2009
Dauler, Catherine G., President .... 01/01/2000 — 12/31/2007
Daubert, Thomas E. .... 01/01/1992 — 12/31/2007
Filippelli, Ronald L. .... 01/10/2006 — 12/31/2009
Goreham, Elizabeth A. .... 01/01/1998 — 12/31/2009
Hahn, Donald M. .... 01/01/2006 — 12/31/2009
Humphrey, Craig R. .... 01/01/2004 — 12/31/2007
Kern, Jeffrey R. .... 01/01/2004 — 12/31/2007
Fountaine, Thomas J., II, Manager ....11/05/2003 — Indefinite Term
Kurtz, Thomas J., Assistant Manager .. 03/20/2006 — Indefinite Term
Dunlap, Roger A., Jr., Assistant Manager ... 10/15/2007 — Indefinite Term
Hanscom, Cynthia S., Assistant Secretary . 04/13/2005 — Indefinite Term
Williams, Terry J., Solicitor .... 1987 — Indefinite Term

2008

Welch, William L., Jr., Mayor .... 01/01/1994 — 12/31/2009
Goreham, Elizabeth A., President .... 01/01/1998 — 12/31/2009
Filippelli, Ronald L. .... 01/10/2006 — 12/31/2009
Hahn, Donald M. .... 01/01/2006 — 12/31/2009
Lafer, Theresa D. .... 01/01/2008 — 12/31/2011
Lawrence, Silvi .... 01/01/2008 — 12/31/2011
Morris, Peter .... 01/01/2008 — 12/31/2011
Rosenberg, James L. .... 01/01/2008 — 12/31/2011
Fountaine, Thomas J., II, Manager ....11/05/2003 — Indefinite Term
Kurtz, Thomas J., Assistant Manager .. 03/20/2006 — Indefinite Term
Dunlap, Roger A., Jr., Assistant Manager ... 10/15/2007 — Indefinite Term
Hanscom, Cynthia S., Assistant Secretary . 04/13/2005 — Indefinite Term
Williams, Terry J., Solicitor .... 1987 — Indefinite Term

2009

Welch, William L., Jr., Mayor (died in office) ... 01/01/1994 — 09/04/2009
Lewis, Felicia, Interim Mayor .... 10/01/2009 — 12/31/2009
Goreham, Elizabeth A., President .... 01/01/1998 — 12/31/2009
Filippelli, Ronald L. .... 01/01/2006 — 12/31/2009
Hahn, Donald M.. 01/01/2006 — 12/31/2009
Lafer, Theresa D. .... 01/01/2008 — 12/31/2011
Lawrence, Silvi.. 01/01/2008 — 12/31/2011
Morris, Peter .... 01/01/2008 — 12/31/2011
Rosenberg, James L. .... 01/01/2008 — 12/31/2011
Fountaine, Thomas J., II, Manager ....11/05/2003 — Indefinite Term
Kurtz, Thomas J., Assistant Manager .. 03/20/2006 — Indefinite Term
Dunlap, Roger A., Jr., Assistant Manager ... 10/15/2007 — Indefinite Term
Ergler, Sharon K., Assistant Secretary   09/08/2009 — Indefinite Term
Williams, Terry J., Solicitor ....1987 — Indefinite Term

2010

Goreham, Elizabeth A., Jr., Mayor .... 01/01/2010 — 12/31/2013
Filippelli, Ronald L., President .... 01/01/2010 — 12/31/2013
Daubert, Thomas E... 01/01/2010 — 12/31/2013
Hahn, Donald M... 01/01/2010 — 12/31/2013
Lafer, Theresa D. .... 01/01/2008 — 12/31/2011
Lawrence, Silvi... 01/01/2008 — 12/31/2011
Morris, Peter .... 01/01/2008 — 12/31/2011
Rosenberg, James L. .... 01/01/2008 — 12/31/2011
Fountaine, Thomas J., II, Manager ....11/05/2003 — Indefinite Term
Kurtz, Thomas J., Assistant Manager .... 03/20/2006 — 07/15/2010
Dunlap, Roger A., Jr., Assistant Manager ... 10/15/2007 — Indefinite Term
Ergler, Sharon K., Assistant Secretary   09/08/2009 — Indefinite Term
Williams, Terry J., Solicitor .... 1987 — Indefinite Term

2011

Goreham, Elizabeth A., Jr., Mayor .... 01/01/2010 — 12/31/2013
Filippelli, Ronald L., President .... 01/01/2010 — 12/31/2013
Daubert, Thomas E. .... 01/01/2010 — 12/31/2013
Hahn, Donald M. .... 01/01/2010 — 12/31/2013
Lafer, Theresa D. .... 01/01/2008 — 12/31/2011
Lawrence, Silvi .... 01/01/2008 — 12/31/2011
Morris, Peter .... 01/10/2008 — 12/31/2011
Rosenberg, James L. .... 01/01/2008 — 12/31/2011
Fountaine, Thomas J., II, Manager ....11/05/2003 — Indefinite Term
Dunlap, Roger A., Jr., Assistant Manager ... 10/15/2007 — Indefinite Term
Ergler, Sharon K., Assistant Secretary 09/08/2009 — Indefinite Term
Williams, Terry J., Solicitor .... 1987 — Indefinite Term

2012

Goreham, Elizabeth A., Jr., Mayor .... 01/01/2010 — 12/31/2013
Hahn, Donald M., President .... 01/01/2010 — 12/31/2013
Daubert, Thomas E. .... 01/01/2010 — 12/31/2013
Dauler, Catherine G. .... 01/01/2012 — 12/31/2015
Filippelli, Ronald L. .... 01/01/2010 — 12/31/2013
Klinetob, Sarah .... 01/01/2012 — 12/31/2015
Morris, Peter .... 01/01/2008 — 12/31/2011
Rosenberg, James L. .... 01/01/2008 — 12/31/2011
Fountaine, Thomas J., II, Manager ....11/05/2003 — Indefinite Term
Dunlap, Roger A., Jr., Assistant Manager ... 10/15/2007 — Indefinite Term
Ergler, Sharon K., Assistant Secretary 09/08/2009 — Indefinite Term
Williams, Terry J., Solicitor .... 1987 — Indefinite Term

2013

Goreham, Elizabeth A., Jr., Mayor .... 01/01/2010 — 12/31/2013
Hahn, Donald M., President .... 01/01/2010 — 12/31/2013
Daubert, Thomas E. .... 01/01/2010 — 12/31/2013
Dauler, Catherine G. .... 01/01/2012 — 12/31/2015
Filippelli, Ronald L. .... 01/01/2010 — 12/31/2013
Klinetob, Sarah .... 01/01/2012 — 12/31/2015
Morris, Peter .... 01/01/2008 — 12/31/2015
Rosenberg, James L. .... 01/01/2008 — 12/31/2015
Fountaine, Thomas J., II, Manager ....11/05/2003 — Indefinite Term
Dunlap, Roger A., Jr., Assistant Manager ... 10/15/2007 — Indefinite Term
Ergler, Sharon K., Assistant Secretary 09/08/2009 — Indefinite Term
Williams, Terry J., Solicitor .... 1987 — Indefinite Term

2014

Goreham, Elizabeth A., Jr., Mayor .... 01/01/2010 — 12/31/2013
Rosenberger, James L., President .... 01/01/2008 — 12/31/2015
Daubert, Thomas E. .... 01/01/2010 — 12/31/2017
Dauler, Catherine G. .... 01/01/2012 — 12/31/2015
Klinetob, Sarah .... 01/01/2012 — 12/31/2015
Lafer, Theresa D. .... 01/01/2014 — 12/31/2017
Morris, Peter .... 01/01/2008 — 12/31/2015
Myers, Evan .... 01/01/2014 — 12/31/2017
Fountaine, Thomas J., II, Manager ....11/05/2003 — Indefinite Term
Dunlap, Roger A., Jr., Assistant Manager ... 10/15/2007 — Indefinite Term
Ergler, Sharon K., Assistant Secretary 09/08/2009 — Indefinite Term
Williams, Terry J., Solicitor .... 1987 — Indefinite Term

2015

Goreham, Elizabeth A., Jr., Mayor .... 01/01/2010 — 12/31/2017
Rosenberger, James L., President.................. 01/01/2008 — 12/31/2015
Daubert, Thomas E.. 01/01/2010 — 12/31/2017
Dauler, Catherine G. .... 01/01/2012 — 12/31/2015
Klinetob, Sarah .... 01/01/2012 — 12/31/2015
Lafer, Theresa D. .... 01/01/2014 — 12/31/2017
Morris, Peter .... 01/01/2008 — 12/31/2015
Myers, Evan .... 01/01/2014 — 12/31/2017
Fountaine, Thomas J., II, Manager ....11/05/2003 — Indefinite Term
Dunlap, Roger A., Jr., Assistant Manager ... 10/15/2007 — Indefinite Term
Ergler, Sharon K., Assistant Secretary 09/08/2009 — Indefinite Term
Williams, Terry J., Solicitor .... 1987 — Indefinite Term

2016

Goreham, Elizabeth A., Jr., Mayor .... 01/01/2010 — 12/31/2017
Daubert, Thomas E., President .... 01/01/2010 — 12/31/2017
Barlow, Jesse L. .... 01/01/2016 — 12/31/2019
Brown, David L. .... 01/01/2016 — 12/31/2019
Dauler, Catherine G. .... 01/01/2012 — 12/31/2019
Engeman, Janet P. .... 01/01/2016 — 12/31/2019
Lafer, Theresa D. .... 01/01/2014 — 12/31/2017
Myers, Evan .... 01/01/2014 — 12/31/2017
Fountaine, Thomas J., II, Manager ....11/05/2003 — Indefinite Term
Dunlap, Roger A., Jr., Assistant Manager ... 10/15/2007 — Indefinite Term
King, Thomas R., Assistant Manager ..... 09/01/2016 — Indefinite Term
Ergler, Sharon K., Assistant Secretary 09/08/2009 — Indefinite Term
Williams, Terry J., Solicitor .... 1987 — Indefinite Term

Council 2016-2017. (Left-to-right) Janet Engeman, Evan Myers, Thomas Daubert (President), Elizabeth Goreham (Mayor), Catherine Dauler, Jesse Barlow, David Brown, and Theresa Lafer. Photo by the Borough of State College.

2017

Goreham, Elizabeth A., Jr., Mayor .... 01/01/2010 — 12/31/2017

Daubert, Thomas E., President .... 01/01/2010 — 12/31/2017

Barlow, Jesse L. .... 01/01/2016 — 12/31/2019

Brown, David L. .... 01/01/2016 — 12/31/2019

Dauler, Catherine G. .... 01/01/2012 — 12/31/2019

Engeman, Janet P. .... 01/01/2016 — 12/31/2019

Lafer, Theresa D. .... 01/01/2014 — 12/31/2017

Myers, Evan .... 01/01/2014 — 12/31/2017

Fountaine, Thomas J., II, Manager ....11/05/2003 — Indefinite Term

Dunlap, Roger A., Jr., Assistant Manager ... 10/15/2007 — Indefinite Term

King, Thomas R., Assistant Manager ..... 09/01/2016 — Indefinite Term

Ergler, Sharon K., Assistant Secretary   09/08/2009 — Indefinite Term

Williams, Terry J., Solicitor .... 1987 — Indefinite Term

2018

Hahn, Donald M., Mayor .... 01/01/2018 — 12/31/2021
Myers, Evan, President.................................. 01/01/2010 — 12/31/2021
Barlow, Jesse L. .... 01/01/2016 — 12/31/2019
Brown, David L. .... 01/01/2016 — 12/31/2019
Dauler, Catherine G. .... 01/01/2012 — 12/31/2019
Engeman, Janet P. .... 01/01/2016 — 12/31/2019
Lafer, Theresa D. .... 01/01/2014 — 12/31/2021
Murphy, Daniel .... 01/01/2014 — 12/31/2021
Fountaine, Thomas J., II, Manager ....11/05/2003 — Indefinite Term
Dunlap, Roger A., Jr., Assistant Manager ... 10/15/2007 — Indefinite Term
King, Thomas R., Assistant Manager ..... 09/01/2016 — Indefinite Term
Ergler, Sharon K., Assistant Secretary   09/08/2009 — Indefinite Term
Williams, Terry J., Solicitor .... 1987 — Indefinite Term

2019

Hahn, Donald M., Mayor .... 01/01/2018 — 12/16/2019
Filippelli, Ronald L., Mayor .... 12/17/2019 — 12/31/2021
Myers, Evan, President.................................. 01/01/2010 — 12/31/2017
Barlow, Jesse L. .... 01/01/2016 — 12/31/2019
Brown, David L. .... 01/01/2016 — 12/31/2019
Dauler, Catherine G. .... 01/01/2012 — 12/31/2019
Engeman, Janet P. .... 01/01/2016 — 12/31/2019
Lafer, Theresa D. .... 01/01/2014 — 12/31/2021
Murphy, Daniel .... 01/01/2014 — 12/31/2021
Fountaine, Thomas J., II, Manager ....11/05/2003 — Indefinite Term
Dunlap, Roger A., Jr., Assistant Manager ... 10/15/2007 — Indefinite Term
King, Thomas R., Assistant Manager ..... 09/01/2016 — Indefinite Term
Ergler, Sharon K., Assistant Secretary   09/08/2009 — Indefinite Term
Williams, Terry J., Solicitor .... 1987 — Indefinite Term

2020

Filippelli, Ronald L., Mayor .... 12/17/2019 — 12/31/2021
Barlow, Jesse L., President .... 01/01/2016 — 12/31/2023
Behring, Deanna... 01/01/2020 — 12/31/2023
Engeman, Janet P. .... 01/01/2016 — 12/31/2023
Lafer, Theresa D. .... 01/01/2014 — 12/31/2021
Marshall, Peter S. .... 01/20/2020 — 12/31/2023
Murphy, Daniel .... 01/01/2014 — 09/03/2021
Myers, Evan .... 01/01/2014 — 12/31/2021
Yeaple, Katherine Oh .... 10/05/2020 — 12/31/2021
Fountaine, Thomas J., II, Manager ....11/05/2003 — Indefinite Term
Dunlap, Roger A., Jr., Assistant Manager ... 10/15/2007 — Indefinite Term
King, Thomas R., Assistant Manager ..... 09/01/2016 — Indefinite Term
Ergler, Sharon K., Assistant Secretary 09/08/2009 — Indefinite Term
Williams, Terry J., Solicitor .... 1987 — Indefinite Term

2021

Filippelli, Ronald L., Mayor .... 12/17/2019 — 12/31/2021
Barlow, Jesse L., President .... 01/01/2016 — 12/31/2023
Behring, Deanna... 01/01/2020 — 12/31/2023
Engeman, Janet P. .... 01/01/2016 — 12/31/2023
Lafer, Theresa D. .... 01/01/2014 — 12/31/2021
Marshall, Peter S. .... 01/20/2020 — 12/31/2023
Myers, Evan .... 01/01/2014 — 12/31/2021
Yeaple, Katherine Oh .... 10/05/2020 — 12/31/2021
Fountaine, Thomas J., II, Manager ....11/05/2003 — Indefinite Term
Dunlap, Roger A., Jr., Assistant Manager ... 10/15/2007 — Indefinite Term
King, Thomas R., Assistant Manager .... 09/01/2016 — 10/31/2021
Ergler, Sharon K., Assistant Secretary .... 09/08/2009 — 10/01/2021
Walter, Dianna, Assistant Secretary ...... 10/27/2021 — Indefinite Term
Williams, Terry J., Solicitor .... 1987 — Indefinite Term

2022

Nanes, Ezra, Mayor .... 01/01/2022 — 12/31/2025
Barlow, Jesse L., President .... 01/01/2016 — 12/31/2023
Balachandran, Gopal .... 01/01/2022 — 12/31/2025
Behring, Deanna... 01/01/2020 — 12/31/2023
Biever, Richard .... 01/01/2022 — 06/13/2022
Engeman, Janet P. .... 01/01/2016 — 12/31/2023
Krishnankutty, Nalini .... 06/22/2022 — 12/31/2023
Lipscomb, Divine R....................................... 01/01/2022 — 12/31/2025
Marshall, Peter S. .... 01/20/2020 — 12/31/2023
Fountaine, Thomas J., II, Manager ....11/05/2003 — Indefinite Term
Dunlap, Roger A., Jr., Assistant Manager ... 10/15/2007 — Indefinite Term
Walter, Dianna, Assistant Secretary ...... 10/27/2021 — Indefinite Term
Williams, Terry J., Solicitor .... 1987 — Indefinite Term

2023

Nanes, Ezra, Mayor .... 01/01/2022 — 12/31/2025
Barlow, Jesse L., President .... 01/01/2016 — 12/31/2023
Balachandran, Gopal .... 01/01/2022 — 12/31/2025
Behring, Deanna... 01/01/2020 — 12/31/2023
Engeman, Janet P. .... 01/01/2016 — 12/31/2023
Krishnankutty, Nalini .... 06/22/2022 — 12/31/2023
Lipscomb, Divine R....................................... 01/01/2022 — 12/31/2025
Marshall, Peter S. .... 01/20/2020 — 12/31/2023
Fountaine, Thomas J., II, Manager ....11/05/2003 — Indefinite Term
Dunlap, Roger A., Jr., Assistant Manager ... 10/15/2007 — Indefinite Term
Walter, Dianna, Assistant Secretary ...... 10/27/2021 — Indefinite Term
Williams, Terry J., Solicitor .... 1987 — Indefinite Term

Council President
1996-2024

Council Presidents are selected by sitting Council Members every two years as membership of Council changes. The first thirty Council Presidents served from 1896 to 1995 for a total time of 100 years. Names are listed in the Addison book. Starting in the 1980s, Council Presidents, by informed agreement, typically do not serve consecutive terms, but could be elected again after a two-year or more hiatus. This arrangement was followed to allow more council members to serve as President during their time on Council.

The president serves mainly as a Chair but represents Council in many ways throughout the community and in the Centre Region Council of Governments (COG), where all elected Council and Township members meet as a group to administer regional programs. The President is the chief executive officer of the Borough, although the Mayor serves as the face of the Borough to many outside groups. Together with the Borough Manager, the President of Council sets items to be considered by Council at any meeting or work session. At each Council meeting, all members may propose items to be discussed at subsequent meetings.

Thomas E. Daubert	1996-1997
Jean W. McManis	1998-1999
Janet K. Knauer	2000-2001
Richard L. McCarl	2001-2003
Thomas E. Daubert	2004-2005
Catherine G. Dauler	2006-2007
Elizabeth A. Goreham	2008-2009

Mayors

1994-2023

Since 1968, Mayors of State College have been elected for four-year terms and can be reelected for four-year terms without limitations. An unexpected vacancy in the office is filled by a vote of Council until the next regular Council two-year election.

Since the Home Rule Charter was adopted in 1973, the Mayor serves as a ceremonial head of the Borough but no longer has any administrative or executive power. The Mayor serves as presiding officer at Council meetings but has no vote on any motions, including legislative ordinances. However, on any ordinance passed by Council, the Mayor, on his own volition, may veto the ordinance and is required to give Council written responses for the veto. The Mayor signs approval of each ordinance that is not vetoed. Council may either accept or, by a 2/3 vote (five or more of the seven members), override the veto and accept the ordinance. The Mayor has no power to veto any other legislation, but can obviously discuss any of his ideas with Council.

The Mayors (earlier called Burgesses) of the Borough of State College from 1896 until 1996 are listed in the Addison book. The Mayors serving from 1996 to 2023 are listed below. Some comments on each are appended.

William L. Welch Jr. 01/01/1994-09/04/2009

Felicia Lewis 10/01/2009-12/31/2009

Elizabeth A. Goreham 01/01/2010-12/31/2017

Donald H. Hahn....................................... 01/01/2018-12/16/2019

Ronald L. Filippelli 12/17/2019-12/31/2021

Ezra Nanes 01/01/2022-Current

William (Bill) Welch served a total of 15 years and was in office until his death in September 2009. He had served on Council for four years before he was elected Mayor after the previous Mayor, Arnold Addison, retired from the post. He represented the Borough with vigor to Penn State and many other organizations in the community. The plaza in front of the Municipal Building was named in his honor.

Felicia Lewis was appointed by Council to complete the term of Mayor Welch. She served as a Council member from 1992 to 1995 and was previously one of the most active ABC members, working diligently and positively for decades.

Elizabeth Goreham served as mayor for two full terms after three terms on Council, including one as Council President. She was an extremely active participant in her mayoral duties, as well as working with a myriad of community groups.

Donald Hahn was elected for a four-year term from 2018 to 2021 but resigned, as required, to take office as a District Judge in State College starting in 2020 and continuing at this writing. He previously served several terms as a Council member, including a two-year term as Council President. In the author's view, he was one of the best prepared on all issues before Council.

Ronald Filippelli was appointed by Council to complete the term of Donald Hahn and served with distinction for the unusual role of Mayor during the first two years of the COVID-19 pandemic. He previously served as a Council member for two terms, with two years as Council President.

Ezra Nanes was elected for his first term from 2022 to 2025.

Mayor William L. Welch Jr.
Photo by the Borough of State College.

Mayor Felicia Lewis
Photo by the Borough of State College.

Mayor Elizabeth Goreham.
Photo by the Borough of State College.

Mayor Donald Hahn.
Photo by the Borough of State College.

Mayor Ronald Filippelli.
Photo by the Borough of State College.

Mayor Ezra Nanes.
Photo by the Borough of State College

Managers

The purpose of the Borough Manager is to be the chief executive of the municipality. All employees of the Borough are approved for employment by the Manager and report to the supervisor of the department in which they are employed. Departments vary somewhat with time but basically include Administration, Finance, Health, Ordinance Enforcement, Parking, Planning, Police, and Public Works. The heads of all departments report to the Borough Manager. An Assistant Manager primarily works on Finance but aids the Manager in other departments. The Assistant Borough Secretary is the chief recorder of minutes and other documents, and also supervises the administrative assistants.

The Borough Manager is appointed by Council for an indeterminate term, subject to a contractual arrangement. Council itself has only two employees, the Borough Manager and the Borough Solicitor. While Council members continuously interact with department heads and other members of staff for purposes of information gathering, Council members do not supervise any members of the staff. Questions asked of staff by Council members are for informational purposes. Any other questions, and definitely any questions involving personnel, must be asked through the Borough Manager.

Only two persons served as Borough Manager from 1996 to the current date, Peter Marshall and Thomas J. Fountaine, II.

Peter Marshall served from September 1986 until he retired in September 2003. His full pedigree from 1986 until early 1996 is given in the Addison book. Since then, he has been instrumental in large projects that were undertaken by the Borough. Donation of land by the Borough and planning of the new Schlow Centre Region Library (formerly Schlow Memorial Library) required much attention. The new Municipal Building, which opened in

2001, was a major accomplishment of the Manager and Council (Description of the building is given in   a later section.) His advocacy for the construction of the building and planning efforts were instrumental in its success. An interview with Peter is contained in a later section of this monograph. An interesting fact is that Peter ran and was elected as a member of Council for the 2020 to 2023 term. He brought a wealth of experience to a Council with many new members.

Thomas J. Fountaine, II has served as Borough Manager since November 2003. He is an Indiana native and graduated from Indiana University. He served as staff for Bedford, Indiana, from 1980 until 1985. He served as Manager of Hollidaysburg, Pennsylvania, from 1985 until he accepted Council's offer from State College in Fall 2003 to become Borough Manager, the position he now holds. He has handled the rapid growth and changes in the community in a superior manner throughout these last 20 years. The Borough government and its over 200 employees, Council, the community members, the cooperative efforts with the other five municipalities in the Centre region, primarily through Council of Governments, Centre County, and Penn State University, have been served very well by his efforts on behalf of the largest borough in Pennsylvania. The Borough's responses to the COVID-19 virus were especially notable. His comments on many important issues considered during his continuing tenure are given in an interview contained later in this volume.

Borough Manager Peter Marshall.

Photo by the Borough of State College.

Borough Manager Tom Fontaine.

Photo by the Borough of State College

Solicitor

Since 1996, only one attorney has served as State College Solicitor, as the appointment runs until relieved by Council, or by resignation or retirement.

Penn State graduate and Dickinson Law School graduate Terry J. Williams has served in this capacity since fall 1987. He attends all regular meetings of Council to make recommendations and to answer questions from Council members. He also represents the Borough in court proceedings where there is no conflict of interest with another attorney in his firm. Another attorney is sometimes hired to represent the Borough in cases that may be long-term or of a specialized nature. He is the prime legal adviser to the Manager, Department Heads, and Council members in matters of Borough authority. He also meets regularly when asked with other members of the administrative staff and individual Council members. His extensive and extremely valuable service to the State College government was recognized by Council through his selection as the Legacy Award recipient in 2017 after 25 years as the State College Solicitor.

Authorities, Boards, Commissions

This chapter provides important information about local and regional authorities, boards, commissions, and committees.

Members of the ABCs serve without compensation. Most are advisory to Borough Council, but certain authorities are lease-operating boards rather than leaseback or advisory authorities. Some other boards have legal standings.

How the Borough's Government Works

The Borough of State College is a home rule municipality, operating under a Council-Manager charter, which determines the structure and operating procedure to be followed by our government.

Under this charter, a seven-member council is the legislative branch of the government. Members are elected at large for four-year, overlapping terms. Council members are not paid. In addition to work sessions, regular meetings are usually held on the first and third Mondays of each month at 7 p.m. in Council Chambers of the Municipal Building. All meetings are open to the public. A prepared agenda is available at the door and on the Borough's website.

An elected Mayor is the ceremonial head of government. In addition, the Mayor serves as the presiding officer at council meetings and has veto power on ordinance actions. Of their own volition, the Mayor may act as a community ombudsman for citizen complaints on certain appeals.

An appointed Manager acts on behalf of Council in administrative and non-legislative matters. The Manager is the executive officer of the government.

The Borough is a member of the Centre Region Council of Governments (COG), organized in 1969. Other COG members are the five surrounding townships of State College: College, Ferguson, Halfmoon, Harris, and Patton townships. COG provides a variety of governmental services for the Centre Region municipalities on a contractual basis. These services include administration, emergency management, code enforcement, recreational programs, short- and long-range regional planning, fire protection, and library facilities.

The Borough is a part of Centre County. At the County level of government, Council appoints representatives to the County's Airport Authority, Solid Waste Authority, and Community Foundation.

Council receives advice from more than 100 appointed residents. Ad hoc committees and quasi-judicial groups account for approximately 30 other volunteers.

Board of Health est. 1914

The Board of Health was created to advise on public health issues. The Board consists of five members who are appointed for a term of five years. At least one member of the Board must be a health professional. The board meets quarterly.

Members of the Board are responsible for enforcing the laws of the Commonwealth, including regulations of the State Department of Health, and all ordinances of the Borough enacted to prevent the introduction and spread of infectious or contagious diseases and protect the environment. Members also offer advice on the existence and abatement of nuisances and make recommendations to Council on rules and regulations necessary for the presentation of public health.

Zoning Hearing Board est. 1927

There are four members of the Zoning Hearing Board (three regular, one alternate), all of whom are appointed for three-year terms. During their tenure, members are not permitted to hold any other municipal office.

The Board is responsible for hearing and deciding appeals. The Zoning Officer applies or interprets the regulations. The Board often makes decisions on special exceptions consistent with the terms of the zoning ordinance. They also authorize variances from the terms of the zoning ordinance as permitted by the state statutes.

Planning Commission est. 1930

The State College Planning Commission is comprised of seven members, each of whom is appointed for a term of four years. The Commission meets on the first Wednesday of the month at noon and on the third Thursday of the month at 7 p.m.

The Commission reviews plans for the development and improvement of the Borough, and prepares policies, regulations, and programs for consideration by Council. Areas of concern include land use, downtown revitalization, neighborhood conservation, open space, beautification, public facilities, and transportation. Duties of the Commission are listed in the Pennsylvania Municipalities Planning Code. The Commission also tries to ensure that singular interests and the overall public welfare follow the adopted Comprehensive Plan. To this end, one member of the Commission serves as a member of the Centre Regional Planning Commission.

Borough Water Authority est. 1940

The Water Authority was created to operate and own the water distribution system for the Borough and other areas that may be authorized by Council to be served. This Authority is charged with planning for the future by developing water resources and encouraging conservation. The Authority is an operating entity with an appointed manager and staff.

Civil Service Commission est. 1941

The Civil Service Commission consists of three residents of the Borough (or municipalities served by the Borough's Police Department) and is appointed for terms of six years.

The Commission has the power to prescribe, amend, and enforce rules and regulations governing police appointments and promotions. The Commission meets infrequently when there is a need for its service.

Authorities Board est. 1954

The current Authorities Board is the culmination of the Industrial & Commercial Development Authority, Municipal Building Authority, Parking Authority, Sewer Authority, Storm Water Authority, and Public Safety Building Authority. The board was created to finance and supervise several construction projects, which required ongoing actions due to the bond issue and indenture requirements.

Design Review Board est. 1970

The Design Review Board consists of seven residents of the Borough who are appointed by Council for four-year terms. The Board routinely meets twice each month.

Members advise Council on matters pertaining to design and historic resources, identify historic resources, advocate for community-sensitive design in new construction, work on the preservation of historic resources, and serve as a clearinghouse for information and education on design and historic resources. The Board also works closely with the Planning Commission.

Tree Commission re-est. 1976

The Tree Commission consists of five Borough resident members, at least two of whom are professionals in forestry, horticulture, plant pathology, entomology, landscape architecture, or related fields. Members are appointed for terms of three years. The Commission meets six times each year, usually during the day.

Members advise on the planning, maintenance, and removal of trees within the public rights-of-way and on other lands within their jurisdiction, and are responsible for a Master Plan for street trees.

The Commission holds hearings when new trees are to be planted and hears appeals from property owners concerning decisions to plant, remove, or treat trees on public or private property.

Community Development Block Grant Citizens' Advisory Committee re-est. 1992

The CDBG Citizens' Advisory Committee consists of seven members who are residents of the Borough. The Committee usually meets on the first Tuesday of the month at noon.

The Committee's primary role is to create a focal point for resident involvement in the spending of the annual block grants and other activities related to the CDBG and HOME programs. The Committee provides residents of State College with an ongoing opportunity to express their views and concerns about neighborhood and community needs that are eligible for CDBG and HOME funding. In performing these tasks, the Committee serves as an advisory body to Council, reviewing and making recommendations on grant proposals and related matters.

Rental Housing Revocation Appeal Board est. 1996

The Rental Housing Revocation Appeal Board is made up of three members and one alternate who are residents of the Borough. Members are appointed by Council to serve three-year terms. Members have exclusive jurisdiction to hear and render adjudications from decisions made by the Manager with respect to the revocation of a rental housing permit. Board members meet infrequently, or when an appeal is filed.

Transportation Commission re-est. 2003

The seven members of the Transportation Commission are residents of the Borough, appointed by Council for four-year terms. Commission members meet on the second Tuesday of each month.

Commission members provide advice to Council on strategies for parking and parking rates and for the implementation of relevant portions of the Transportation Policy. Members also discuss and recommend programs that encourage and accommodate the use of alternative transportation programs.

Redevelopment Authority est. 2006

The Redevelopment Authority consists of five members appointed by the Mayor for four-year terms. Members must be residents of the Borough.

The Borough created this authority to encourage safe and convenient services, housing stock, a decent living environment, and adequate places of employment and commercial activity for the citizens of the Borough and the community at large.

Real Estate Advisory Committee est. 2015

The Real Estate Advisory Committee was established to assist staff and the Redevelopment Authority with program evaluation of the Housing Investment Program (HIP). The REAC consists of five members and usually meets twice per year.

Dr. Martin Luther King Jr. Plaza Committee est. 2016

The committee project began in 2012, when former Borough Council Member Peter Morris led the motion to pass Resolution 1066, the renaming of Fraser Plaza to Dr. Martin Luther King Jr. Plaza. Established in 2016, the committee was originally charged with reviewing and making recommendations to Borough Council on the design, content, and installation of commemorative elements within Dr. Martin Luther King Jr. Plaza. The Plaza opened on August 28, 2017, the 54th anniversary of the 1963 March on Washington for Jobs and Freedom, where Dr. King first gave his "I Have a Dream" speech. The Committee continues to meet to discuss plaza enhancements and events.

LGBTQ+ Advisory Commission est. 2017

In 2017, the State College Borough Council established the Lesbian, Gay, Bisexual, Transgender, and Queer (LGBTQ+) Advisory Commission to advise the Borough on LGBTQ+ matters.

Historical Architectural Review Board est. 2018

In 2017, the Historical Architectural Review Board was created to oversee regulated activities within the Holmes Foster/Highlands and College Heights historic districts. The HARB historic districts protect the quality of the architecture in the districts and safeguard architectural heritage by establishing a thoughtful review process for some changes to the exterior of buildings to prevent hasty or inappropriate alterations or demolition. New construction and additions are assessed according to how the proposed change will affect the appearance of a building or the overall character of a street, and whether significant architectural features will be hidden, damaged, or lost.

Community Oversight Board est. 2021

The Community Oversight Board was created in 2021 by the State College Borough Council to provide oversight of the State College Police Department to ensure that everyone who lives, works, studies in, or visits State College may live safely and experience equitable treatment in their interactions with the police.

Racial Equity Advisory Commission est. 2023

The Racial Equity Advisory Commission was established in January 2023 by the State College Borough Council to assist and advise the Borough of State College on policies, practices, procedures, and programs using a racial equity lens. The Commission serves as a forum for public discussions and input on the various racial equity matters under the Commission's purview. Additionally, the Commission engages in outreach and programming related to its purpose and charge.

Regional Human Relations Commission re-est. 2024

The Human Relations Commission was established in 2008 and consists of five residents of the Borough or the Centre Region. Members are appointed by Council to serve three-year terms. The commission was created to hear and adjudicate complaints filed in relation to the Anti-Discrimination Ordinance. The Human Relations Commission meets as needed.

Regional Government ABCs

Schlow Centre Regional Library Board of Trustees est. 1955

The Schlow Centre Region Library Board, established in accordance with the Pennsylvania Library Code, is responsible for making policy for the Library and for overseeing Library operations.

The Library is a regional agency of COG, currently funded jointly by the Borough of State College and four of the townships. The nine-member Board of Trustees includes two residents of the Borough, appointed in accordance with the COG Joint Articles of Agreement. Members serve a maximum of two three-year terms. Library Board members meet on the second Wednesday of each month in the evening.

Centre Region Parks and Recreation Authority est. 1970

The Centre Region Parks and Recreation Authority has six members, two of whom are appointed by Council to represent State College and the State College Area School District. Members serve for a term of five years. Since some members also serve on ad hoc committees, a typical Authority member may attend approximately 15 meetings per year.

The Authority acts in advisory capacity to determine policy and programs for the Parks and Recreation Department and oversees implementation of these policies and programs within the limits established by an approved COG budget.

The Centre Regional Recreation Authority operates the William L. Welch and Park Forest Outdoor Swimming Pools. The Authority meets on the third Thursday of each month.

Centre Area Transportation Authority est. 1982

The Centre Area Transportation Authority (CATA) is a regional authority, overseen by a five-member Board of Directors, which sets policy for its staff. Each of the five member municipalities (including the Borough of State College) appoints one member to the Board. CATA usually meets on the fourth Monday of each month at 4 p.m.

CATA operates a fixed route regional bus service called Centre Line. Members also oversee Centre Ride, a complimentary, demand-responsive, para-transit service for the elderly and disabled. Fixed route and para-transit services are also provided to non-members. Municipalities on a contractual basis. In addition, CATA operates Loops and Links services for those who commute from outside CATA's service area.

Centre Network (C-NET) est. 1998

The Board is comprised of one member from each entity sponsoring the public network of a private government channel and an educational channel. The Board is responsible for making all policy and financial decisions to be carried out by the staff of the network.

Centre Regional Building and Housing Board of Appeals

The Board is comprised of five core members, each of whom must be a registered architect, professional engineer, or general contractor. Additional specialist members are added to hear appeals involving disability access, plumbing, mechanical or electrical systems, or existing structure compliance. Members are chosen based on technical training, expertise, or experience. Council endorses appointments to the Board. The Board meets on call when an appeal has been made.

The Board of Appeals was established to assure a uniform interpretation of the International Building and Rental Codes. These Codes are administered by the Centre Region Code Administration Agency, a division of COG. Members conduct hearings on appeals from individuals aggrieved by Code interpretations.

Mental Health Task Force

The Task Force was jointly established by Centre County and the Borough of State College to recommend enhancements to, and identify strengths of, the mental health crisis delivery system in Centre County. Specifically, the Task Force is tasked to examine the continuum of mental health crisis services, including Mobile Crisis Services, Delegate Crisis Services, Involuntary Commitment Warrant Procedures, Police Officers' role in responding to mental health calls, 302 Warrant Procedures, Emergency Department Procedures, and Post-Emergency Department Services.

Regional Tax Appeals Board

The Regional Tax Appeals Board was established under Act 50, the Local Taxpayers' Bill of Rights, to hear appeals of all local taxes. One member or one alternate member is appointed by Council to serve over a five-year period. The Board meets infrequently, only when an appeal is submitted.

Other Groups with Members Appointed by the State College Borough Council

Centre County Airport Authority

Centre County Community Foundation

Centre County Solid Waste Authority

State College Community Land Trust

University Area Joint Authority

Centre County Housing and Land Trust

Centre County Recycling and Refuse Authority

Downtown State College Improvement District

Spring Creek Watershed Commission

Local Government Actions and Activities

This section records the significant, non-annual actions taken and their perceived effects on the Community. General yearly actions on budget, maintenance, capital items, and planning are only discussed for items of lasting or unusual significance.

1996

The Borough's Centennial in 1996 was a very active year on all fronts. The Centennial celebration was a major activity and is discussed in a separate section of this monograph. Among the dozens of other actions and projects taken by the Borough government, some of the major actions in 1996 are noted below.

A continuing program to mark historic properties in the Borough neighborhoods of at least 50 years of age began. Through the program, owners of buildings can request and finance permanent bronze plaques to be installed on the front of their properties. This program remains active.

The Borough of State College took the lead in expanding and renovating the Borough-owned Public Safety Building, 400 West Beaver Avenue, the headquarters of the regional Alpha Fire Company. Although the other Centre Region municipalities chose not to financially support this capital project, they later agreed to finance future maintenance and changes to the building.

An ordinance was enacted to provide for the revocation of a rental housing permit when a property is repeatedly identified as a source of ordinance and/or code violations. This legislation has been revised and supplemented many times over the past 20 years as discussed elsewhere in this monograph.

The Community Land Trust was established to provide housing using federal and community development funds. This program has endured and has been expanded to date to provide homeowner housing to federally qualified persons at costs lower than market value, with the land remaining in trust by the program. Over 40 properties now exist from the program.

The Borough began a study to assess the need for expansion or replacement of the Schlow Memorial Library building – the former U.S. Post Office at the southeast corner of South Allen Street and East Beaver Avenue. Fruition of this project is discussed in a later year.

1997-1999

The year 1997 was a busy time for Borough government. Early in the year, the 200-odd-numbered block of South Allen Street south of the library and Highland Alley was purchased to construct a Town Center to house the municipal offices, a community/arts facility, and possibly the library. However, the land was only used to construct the new Municipal Building in 2001. (Concurrently, the new library was built by COG in 2005 on the site of the existing library and the vacated section of Highland Alley.)

A Historic Resources Commission was created to review land development plans for historic sites in the Holmes-Foster/Highlands and College Heights federal historic neighborhoods. The function of this Commission is now a part of the Design Review Board.

A space separation requirement limiting the number of student rentals in R-2 and R-3 districts by creating a minimum property separation requirement was passed by Council. This action was in addition to the existing three unrelated maximum residency restrictions.

Traffic mitigation changes, including two traffic diverters and a cul-de-sac in East College Heights, were made permanent. The Borough was challenged by Ferguson Township for the closing of North Allen Street at the Borough-Ferguson Township line. This issue remained under consideration by the Centre County Court of Common Pleas.

University Drive was reconstructed and modified from South Atherton Street to Nimitz Avenue.

Many water authorities in Pennsylvania were being sold to private companies for one-time large influxes of money to the municipality that established the Authority. It was learned that the State College Borough Water Authority assets could be sold without Council's approval. Council began selecting the members of the Authority, setting a model for appointing knowledgeable members.

Much discussion took place around this topic, including the possibility of dissolving the Authority and taking over its assets to prevent a sale.

The current excellent operation and oversight of the system made selling the Authority unattractive to Council. Discussions led to an approved plan to continue the Authority and prevent any sale without Council approval. This was followed by discussions on adding two members to the five-member authority from townships using the State College Water Authority services.

Council approved continuous annual partial funding of the Downtown State College Partnership and inclusion of funds for downtown improvement in the Capital Improvement Program.

The Borough of State College and Ferguson Township hosted the 98th annual Pennsylvania League of Cities and Municipalities (now the Pennsylvania Municipal League) Convention. Representatives of member municipalities' governing bodies attended meetings and activities. Borough elected and staff officials were the host arrangements committee for the very well-attended and informative sessions.

Savings over the life of a loan of half a million dollars by retiring old loans of ten million dollars and securing a new loan at a fixed rate of 4.2% began in 1998.

The Commonwealth of Pennsylvania approved the expansion of the State College Borough Water Authority from five Borough residents to seven total members by allowing appointments of two additional members, one each from Patton and Ferguson Townships.

Council is committed to the development of a new municipal building on the 200 block of South Allen Street with the appointment of a Citizens' Advisory Committee. The Committee was co-chaired by council members Jean W. McManis and Thomas E. Daubert. Completion was targeted for 2001. In addition, staff were asked to present recommendations for building a new parking structure (later, the building of the Beaver Avenue Parking Garage). The property at 236 S. Allen St. was purchased to develop a walkway from the new Municipal building to Central Parklet (later renamed Sidney Friedman Park).

Work began on building a new library serving the Centre Region with the appointment by COG and the Schlow Library Board of a committee to identify sites and propose an intermunicipal agreement.

Downtown street furniture was installed with permanent benches purchased by sponsors and trash receptacles and other items purchased by the Borough.

On Saturday, July 12, 1998, near the conclusion of the Central Pennsylvania Festival of the Arts, about 2,000 persons rioted in the 200-300 blocks of East Beaver Avenue after confrontation began among apartment residents on balconies and passersby. Destruction of streetlights, furniture, and other items occurred, with some being burned in the street. Police from the Centre Region and the State worked for 2.5 hours to disperse the crowd. This situation led to 17 arrests mostly identified by security cameras. Staff, Council, and University personnel worked throughout the year to prevent future incidents of this type.

The 1997 challenge by Ferguson Township of the State College East College Heights traffic diverters was decided in favor of the Borough by the Centre County Court of Common Pleas. An appeal to the Pennsylvania Commonwealth Court was made by the Township and was pending at year's end. After discussion Council decided not to change the diverter configuration at this time.

The required 90-day public notice before razing historic buildings in residential districts was extended to the R-3H zoning district.

Council supported a COG report to establish two new satellite fire stations to supplement the Alpha Fire Company station at 400 West Beaver Avenue, at the intersection with South Atherton Street. The stations were to be in Patton and College Townships in or adjacent to the township municipal buildings, and were scheduled for completion in 2000.

Work continued by Council and Planning staff to develop a new zoning district, the University Planned District (UPD), for university lands in State College, Ferguson Township, and College Township. Completion was scheduled for 1999.

Council renamed Small Alley in East College Heights to Lehman Way after Ross B. Lehman, a longtime resident and head of the PSU Alumni Association.

A new bicycle path was installed through Orchard Park and the school district property from Bayberry Drive to the start of South Gill Street.

The Centennial historic photo collection was donated to the Centre County Historical Society to be properly preserved at the Centre Furnace Mansion and made available for research, exhibitions, and publications.

Discussions began in 1999 to address traffic problems on North Atherton Street and on Park Avenue. Other than a change in signal timings and changes in turning lanes, revised traffic patterns were all that could be done for the amount of space available at the time. This was due to the tremendous growth of Atherton Street and its surroundings because of business development in Ferguson, Patton, and Halfmoon Townships to the north.

The previous trailer park land at 1700 S. Atherton St. was in development, requiring the protection of the adjacent Slab Cabin Run.

The Dank's building at 148 S. Allen St. (at the corner with Beaver Avenue) was in the process of renovations for commercial, residential, and a performing theater.

Planning for the new Municipal Building was a major task for Council. The planning continued throughout the year, with a contract to be rewarded by year's end (approved Dec. 31, 1999) and removal of current buildings in early 2000.

Zoning requirements were changed to allow the rebuilding of existing structures within the existing footprint, with the same height restrictions and approval of any changes outside the footprint. In addition, a height limit of 45 feet was placed on buildings in the major business district on College Avenue and on South Allen Street to Highland Alley. The requirement for the remainder of the business district remained at 65 feet.

The University Planned District zoning ordinance discussed in 1998 took effect in 1999.

Neighborhood development plans for State College South, Penfield, and Nittany Hills East were approved for the future to join the previous plans for College Heights, Highlands, and Holmes-Foster neighborhoods.

Federal funds from CDBG and HOME through the State College Community Land Trust were used for conducting a service area needs assessment and for rehabilitating eligible properties and infrastructure. Using these funds, as well as Borough funds, the low and moderate income was increased for seven properties to a total of 17 properties on the tax roll.

New state legislation caused Council to adopt a Taxpayer Bill of Rights and a process for taxpayers to appeal assessment decisions. The establishment of a Regional Appeals Board was approved.

The Alpha Fire Company celebrated its 100th anniversary in 1999 by bringing back the carnival on South Allen Street and the annual parade.

Council approved a resolution to allocate $25,000 per year for 2000-2002 to the new First Night Celebration to be held each December 31.

2000-2002

January 2000 saw the submission of the first report of the Business Privilege Tax Committee, working with a charge that stated that real estate taxes or earned income tax could not be changed in order to eliminate the business privilege tax. The committee was limited in its recommendations, most of which had been previously attempted. Their conclusion was that local tax reform had to be addressed at the state level before the business privilege tax could be replaced.

The rapid expansion of the Penn State University campus to west of Atherton Street caused concern for Council because of possible traffic connections to North Gill, North Sparks, and North Patterson Streets. Council reserved its right to rigorously control traffic if such streets were opened to University land.

Bonds were issued for $8 million for construction of the new Municipal Building. Bids were awarded for $8.4 million. Completion and occupancy were expected in December 2001.

A new COG office building, to be built in Ferguson Township near CATO Park, was approved by all Centre Region municipalities. The new facility will contain Planning, Code Administration, Parks and Recreation, and Administration offices.

Council conditionally endorsed the University Area Joint Authority plan to implement a beneficial reuse water system for the region. Plans remained to be finalized.

To encourage the Schlow Memorial Library (now the Schlow Centre Region Library) to remain downtown, Council offered to purchase the Fox Building (Centre Hardware) and to vacate a portion of Highland Alley to provide additional space for expansion of the current library site. This construction was under consideration by the Schlow Library Board.

Council convened a Long-Range Financial Planning Committee, composed of Council members, to review historical data and to make five-year projections as well as evaluate the current mix of taxes and other income-producing sources.

The first positive discussion and partial funding of a skate park was held.

Many plans of the University, most of which required approval, were discussed in 2001. The Skywalk Way to the IST building across North Atherton Street was approved.

A housing project for graduate students on East Campus, the extension of Curtin Road to North Atherton Street, a new street, White Course Drive, connecting Atherton Street with the west campus academic buildings, a surface parking area, and a bicycle trail along the golf course were also approved by Council.

A franchise agreement to transfer the AT&T Broadband Network to Adelphia Communications Corporation was made for a nominal fee, as required, to continue the use of the Borough's rights-of-way.

Traffic calming procedures began for the Highlands neighborhood by limiting access in both directions between East Foster Avenue and University Drive.

Zoning amendments were made that required the land to be reclaimed if a construction project is started and abandoned, that certain principals be named when applying for development plan approvals, and that a traffic impact study for developments of any size that will generate a specified threshold of vehicle trips.

Land on South Allen Street, acquired by the Borough purchase, was donated to Schlow for the construction of the new library.

Late in 2001, the Historic Resources Commission forwarded a proposal for establishing a local historic district in portions of the Borough. Approval would be required for razing or making major changes to historic properties in the district. Discussions were to continue in 2002.

The last week of 2001 showed that the new Municipal Building at 243 S. Allen St. was available for occupancy. Staff proceeded to move to the new facility, discussed in some detail later in this monograph.

The first official Council meeting in the new Municipal Building was held on Jan. 7, 2002. At this meeting, the Downtown State College Improvement District was finalized. Council appointed the first nine-member board to get this private/public partnership started. Governing documents were created, and publications and publicity banners, as well as the beginning of a service to clean all downtown sidewalks, were some initial projects. Planning a vision for the future was a major effort throughout the year.

The first section of new and traditional 'acorn' type streetlights for downtown was installed on South Allen Street to replace the deteriorating lights currently in service. All central downtown streetlights were to be replaced over the next several years.

The approved regional decision to locate the new library at the current site at the corner of East Beaver Avenue and South Allen Street moved forward after much discussion and controversy. In the period of construction, the library was set to move to the former Borough building on South Fraser Street.

Council began discussion about the installation of surveillance cameras in the Calder Way and East Beaver Avenue area to help deter crime and prevent riots. Perpetrators would then be more easily identified. Council was poised to issue a Request for Proposal (RFP) for the purchase and installation of cameras.

Early in 2002, Council agreed to participate in the construction of a COG building at 2643 Gateway Drive in Ferguson Township. Construction began and was scheduled for completion in mid-2003.

Council considered a recommendation to create a local historic district ordinance and held several public meetings to share information with citizens. Council passed an ordinance to create the district in September 2002. Mayor William (Bill) Welch vetoed the ordinance. Council did not attempt to override the veto, which would take five of the seven Council members to do so.

The State College Area School District submitted a waste plan for updating and replacing facilities in January 2002. Council asked that the retention of neighborhood schools and of Memorial Field be important parts of the plan. Council's recommendations were made a part of the final plan by the School Board.

COG Parks and Recreation completed an aquatics study recommending that Welch Pool be retired and replaced by an outdoor seasonal aquatics center. Council objected, citing that the heavy use of the pool and the cost of relocation indicated that the new construction should take place at the current location. This recommendation was under consideration at year's end.

As a result of the Sept. 11, 2001, terrorist attacks, the Borough, together with the other Centre Region municipalities and Penn State, agreed to establish and share the cost of employing a full-time Emergency Management Coordinator.

The year 2002 was an unusually busy time for the Borough in carrying out a myriad of Public Works projects for infrastructure improvement.

2003-2004

The year 2003 saw a continuation of many projects to preserve the infrastructure of the Borough. A major area was stormwater improvements, including the Memorial Field sinkhole (financed by the Borough) in conjunction with the School District project to replace the stone wall surrounding the field and replace the surface of the field with artificial turf. Standards for bicycle paths, replacement of additional light standards, and resurfacing of streets were also approved.

In line with Pennsylvania law, every municipality in the state was required to adopt an emergency operations plan. State College, together with other Centre Region municipalities and Penn State, adopted an approved plan which will be administered by a regional Emergency Management Coordinator.

The Centre Region Metropolitan Planning Organization (MPO) was recommended to be expanded to a county-wide body, and Council agreed. However, implementation was delayed until financial considerations could be resolved.

Early in the year, Council approved a Vision and Strategic Plan for the future of the downtown area to replace a 1990 document. A broader base of traditional retail, a concentration of civic functions, cultural events, and owner-occupied residential condos and townhouses were suggested. Some new facilities in the planning stage were a PSU downtown theater and a summer concert series sponsored by the Downtown State College Improvement District. The vision was considered a long-range plan.

Traffic congestion caused by delivery trucks downtown on College and Beaver Avenues and traffic calming measures throughout the Borough were both discussed with both permanent and temporary methods being studied and attempted.

The new system of requiring trash to be placed at the curb was implemented in March.

The use of surveillance cameras downtown was advanced with the purchase of cameras for use on East Beaver Avenue between McAllister and Hiester Streets. Use began in September 2003, and procedures to be followed were advanced by a Council-appointed oversight committee.

Centre Region COG offices moved to the new building in 2003.

The Senior Center at 131 S. Fraser St. was expanded with funding from all COG entities.

The Commission for Pedestrian and Traffic Safety and the Transportation Commission were combined.

An ordinance was enacted to establish a local training program for servers of alcohol.

An ordinance was passed to require sprinkler systems, like those in rental properties, in fraternity houses over the next five years. The requirement was deemed necessary to provide safety procedures and was agreed to by fraternity advisers.

The reign of Peter Marshall as State College Borough Manager ended mid-year in 2003 after over 17 years of service. Ronald Davis, Assistant Manager, served as Acting Manager until November, at which time the current Borough Manager, Thomas J. Fountaine, II, was hired by Council after a national search. Fountaine came from service as Manager of Hollidaysburg, Pennsylvania.

In 2004, parking was a major discussion topic of Council. In a community where thousands of vehicles enter the Borough and the University each day, as well as the need for parking on many visitor days such as football games, graduations, Arts Festival, etc., parking has always been a concern to Borough citizens.

Council received a study that stated that more parking was needed in the west business area. A municipal parking structure was approved to be constructed at the southwest corner of West Beaver Avenue and South Fraser Street. Such construction required the Borough to buy or negotiate agreements with five land parcels on the construction site, as well as to vacate a small portion of Highland Alley. Other parking discussions included the necessity of making the McAllister Deck more usable and the consideration of more parking facilities in the eastern part of the business district.

Traffic studies were also on a busy burner. The Borough suggested some changes in traffic signals, which were not approved by the state at this time.

Additional bicycle lanes were marked on South Garner Street and Foster Avenue.

Use of the former Borough Building and adjoining sites between Calder Way and West Beaver Avenue led to redevelopment options including a multiscreen cinema.

Council requested the Planning Commission to develop standards for the redevelopment of the Urban Village District, which included the area west of South Atherton Street to the Borough line, south of the Penn State golf courses, and north of West Beaver Avenue. As the area abuts Ferguson Township on the west, discussions ensued on what direction to take.

Stormwater problems were addressed on the school district land on Westerly Parkway and some neighborhoods in the area, as well as additional work at Memorial Field. Such work continued throughout the year.

C-NET's local government and education television channels expanded their service by allowing the deliberations of advisory boards and commissions in addition to their coverage of municipal and school legislative bodies.

In March, State College Borough and Penn State began to allow the University's auxiliary police officers to patrol downtown State College. These officers would refer any serious problems to the regular State College Police. This program continues and has been very successful.

Design of a permanent pedestrian walkway on South Allen Street across from the Municipal Building to end at Central Parklet was approved by Council with completion scheduled for 2005.

Low-level streetlights were installed along South Garner Street from East Beaver Avenue to Hamilton Avenue to increase safety in a very highly traveled student pedestrian area.

Construction of the new Schlow Centre Region Library, including the East Beaver Avenue expanded bus stop and satellite office. Construction was scheduled for completion in August 2005.

The University purchased the land on North Atherton Street north of Railroad Avenue and south of the Information Science and Technology Building for constructing a mixed-use facility of shops, offices, and residences. One contentious point was whether the intercity bus station owned by the University but managed by the Borough should be moved to a site further west. (This plan has been discussed often but, as of 2023, has not begun.)

Uniform building codes were mandated by the State of Pennsylvania in 1999, effective in July 2004. Rather than defer code enforcement to the County, Council decided to enforce all codes through the Centre Region Code Administration Agency of Council of Governments, which also added Halfmoon Township to State College and the four surrounding Townships already members of the Agency.

In 2005, State College again hosted the 105th annual conference of the Pennsylvania League of Cities and Municipalities at the Penn Stater Hotel. Arrangements, hospitality, and non-business financing were provided by the Borough with council members and staff serving as the local committee.

2005-2006

An ad hoc committee was appointed in January to make changes in the tax structure to shift the burden away from single-family properties to properties where a large amount of Borough services are required. The Committee recommended and Council acted to repeal the Business Privilege Tax and adopt the Homestead Exclusion. This latter action allows Council to provide qualified single-family homeowners with a tax assessment reduction to reduce their property taxes in most cases even when property taxes are increased. This shifts more of the property tax burden from owner-occupied single-family homes to rental properties. This exclusion was later adopted by other municipal and educational taxing bodies.

The completion of the Schlow Centre Region Library and the Beaver Avenue Parking Facility were promoted and supported by Council. A bond was issued to cover the cost of the land purchased for land donated to the Centre Region Library, the Beaver Avenue municipal parking facility, and the Westerly Parkway stormwater project.

The Fraser Centre Development to be constructed in the 100 block of Fraser Street on the site of the old Municipal Building and parking lot and the Medical Arts Building was an exciting and challenging major project in 2005. The Borough entered into an agreement with the Downtown State College Improvement District to redevelop the

site for residential, condominium, and cinema uses. Work on the entire Downtown Plan, including areas on College Avenue west of Atherton Street, continued.

In 2006, Council continued its work on Borough-wide projects such as neighborhood quality of life issues and downtown development and enhancement. Zoning updates were sometimes required in this work.

Neighborhood projects of lasting significance included a Holmes-Foster Park Master Plan produced by PSU students; Safety concerns led to the installation of pedestrian countdown/audible signals on Allen Street; bicycle crossing signals at McKee Street and Park Avenue; and West Park Avenue reconstruction.

The downtown Fraser Street/Fraser Centre Street alignment project continued. A Redevelopment Authority, as mandated by state legislation, was established with members appointed by the Mayor. The feasibility of a municipal wireless system to provide a community broadband network to improve government efficiency and make downtown more computer-friendly to residents was evaluated. An assessment of our efforts and needs for recycling and energy conservation, with implementation strategies, was begun with completion scheduled for 2007.

2007-2008

Some highlights of Council's accomplishments for 2007 included the construction of an East/West Bike path on Foster Avenue, approval of the final plans for West End Revitalization, and major work on the Fraser Centre Project. Tasks for implementing the priorities and actions of the West End Plan included preparing new land development regulations, identifying partnerships for redevelopment, creating a redevelopment area, and preparing a capital improvement program. The Fraser Centre redevelopment area and Increment Financing District was approved, with planning on the project continuing with the Downtown State College Improvement District. Expansion of the Commercial Incentive zoning district to the 400 block of East College Avenue to allow buildings to be built to a maximum height of 65 feet was approved by Council.

In 2007, Council adopted an Anti-Discrimination in Employment Ordinance, endorsed a National Citizen Survey, and passed a resolution promoting State College as a Climate Protection Community.

During 2008 Borough Council, in addition to addressing usual annual needs, Council considered various areas of community concern, expanded efforts to 'green' borough operations, continued important areas of redevelopment, continued its cooperative efforts with other Centre Region municipalities, and addressed the Borough's long-term financial health.

The establishment of a Human Relations Commission to address problems of individual discrimination was an important step in the Borough's ongoing efforts to be at the forefront of policies for an all-inclusive community. A program to welcome new students and other new residents to the community each fall began and continues in various forms. Additionally, the State College Police Department achieved professional accreditation, and the Borough gained national recognition as one of the nation's safest communities.

The Fraser Centre project was given approval to submit a final land development plan. The land was transferred to the developer through the Redevelopment Authority, which moved the previously non-taxable area to the tax rolls. Construction was scheduled to begin in 2009. A study of proposed zoning and design regulations for the West End revitalization was begun by the Planning Commission.

The financial health of the Borough was considered on several fronts. The Borough was almost entirely built out and had 47% tax-exempt property in 2008, as well as having a large proportion of non-taxable (mainly student) residents.

Solutions for the future were necessary as both the property and earned income taxes, essentially the only taxes of substance allowed by State law, were flat. Solutions involving both internal cost containment, influence on changing State laws to give municipalities a more diverse menu of allowable taxes, and cooperation with other Centre Region municipalities with common fiscal needs were considered.

2009-2010

The year 2009 included several unexpected changes in the Mayor's position with the passing of Mayor Bill Welch in September after 15 years in office. Felicia Lewis, a very active member of the community for over 30 years at the time and a past Council member, was appointed Mayor by Council to complete the year, with a new Mayor to be elected to take office in 2010.

In 2009, Council approved a completed comprehensive strategic planning process. Six long-term strategic goals with community conservation as the overarching goal were included. The six areas were Neighborhoods, Public Spaces and Infrastructure, Partnerships, Housing, Revitalization, and Operational Sustainability. ABCs, Council, and Borough staff began working to achieve goals in each of these areas.

Neighborhood affordable living needs were addressed by working with the Temporary Housing Foundation and the State College Community Land Trust. 'Student home' definitions were changed to include any house occupied by students with or without the owner on site, making a home separation requirement applicable to all such properties.

An important long-lasting public space change included the rededication of Central Parklet to be renamed Sidney Friedman Park in honor of the long-time business and commercial property owner. Friedman contributed much to the community by donating the State Theatre and other properties for community use. A park stage with a canopy was installed for all-weather use for concerts and other outdoor staged activities.

Council, along with other Centre Region municipalities, committed considerable finances for the complete reconstruction of the William Welch Sr. Community Swimming Pool, originally constructed in the late 1950s, on Westerly

Parkway. The complex has a children's pool and an adult lap pool, both of which are capable of being used for many activities.

The Borough, together with the other Centre Region municipalities and the University, established a permanent full-time Emergency Management Coordinator position with a headquarters at Beaver Stadium on campus.

State College enjoyed recognition from State and National sources for many accomplishments. The Borough was named the second safest community in the United States in City Crime Rankings. Also in 2009, the Borough received the Excellence in Victim Services Award, given only to five communities by the International Association of Chiefs of Police. Also, the Arbor Day Foundation named State College as a Tree City USA to honor its commitment to community forestry. The Borough was honored by this national recognition for the 25th year.

The primary goal for 2009 was identified as neighborhood sustainability because of the strategic plan. New programs improved neighborhood relationships and initiatives by working more closely with the leaders of the various citizen organizations in the Borough. Programs were developed to enhance the enforcement of regulations and ordinances for problem properties and rental housing.

The Borough was selected as the earned income tax collector for all Centre County municipalities and school districts, replacing individual municipal tax collectors. This change was a result of a new state law to improve revenues and services.

After much discussion, a Penn State University undergraduate student representative to Council was appointed to attend all meetings of Council to provide a bridge between the Borough government and the student population. The non-voting member is nominated by the University Park Undergraduate Association and is approved by Council. This position remains today and establishes a clear line of communication with students.

Much discussion ensued on the Fraser Center Development which was delayed because of the recession, but was set to continue in 2011.

Curbside collection of food waste began early in 2010 for Borough residents. The program collected over 500 tons of organic waste in 2010. An augmented system continues to date.

2011-2012

During 2011, public improvements were high-importance items on Council agendas. These included the establishment of the Wetland Education Area in the flood control area on the northern area adjoining Westerly Parkway, just west of South Atherton Street.

Paths and identification markers were installed in this permanent open area. The installation of many ADA-compliant curbs and ramps were undertaken as part of improvements for citizens with disabilities as mandated as a long-term project by state and federal legislation.

The realignment of the 100 block of South Fraser Street was completed next to the Fraser Street Parking Garage and the planned plaza north of the garage.

Housing issues included inclusionary housing legislation to attempt to increase the availability of workforce housing. Included was increased financial support for such programs. Council revised the student home definition to reduce the likelihood of new student rentals in the Borough's stable residential neighborhoods.

In cooperation with the Penn State Student Affairs office, student government, and organizations such as fraternities and sororities, the Living in One Neighborhood (LION) Walk program was carried out in late August to welcome new residents and students to the community. The program was expanded to include a wide swath of student-heavy neighborhoods.

The Neighborhood and Alcohol Team (NEAT) patrols by Borough and University police, as well as student auxiliary officers, were carried out every Thursday, Friday, and Saturday evening. The expanded program was made permanent to reduce crime and enforce ordinances on noise, alcohol, and other violations.

On Oct. 1, 2011, Borough Council dedicated the plaque in front of the Municipal Building, naming the area the Mayor Welch Plaza in honor of the late Mayor.

In 2012, a new refuse ordinance in the Borough with roll-out containers for refuse (mandated) and for organics (not mandated) purchased by the Borough for residents' use was made. Recycling services by the county's solid waste authority remained the same.

Council discussed the effect of the large housing project named 'The Retreat' on Waupelani Drive and its effects on Borough traffic, especially in this section of town. Only about 10% of the land in the project is in the Borough, but all the traffic entering and exiting the project flows through the Borough on Waupelani Drive.

The Fraser Plaza was renamed the D r . Martin Luther King, J r . Plaza by Council to take effect at the conclusion of the plaza's improvements.

Police discussions and legislation included the redefinition of noise violations as ordinance violations rather than disorderly conduct citations. This change was deemed necessary because the public, including most of Council, had different connotations of the meaning and severity of disorderly conduct and noise. The Police Department also began a program of Restorative Justice procedures for citations of limited severity.

The Centre Region Planning Department's document and map of their recommendations for areas of future development in the Borough were discussed with Council, leading to major disagreements as to the effect on neighborhoods. After several iterations, Council approved a new map which preserved neighborhoods in State College.

Discussion of Borough neighborhoods with representatives of the seven organized areas was ongoing and continued with issues on rentals, including 'football rentals,' zoning, student rentals, student homes permits, and ordinance enforcement.

Financing for major work on flood control, including flooding at Memorial Field largely by the flow of rainwater through the adjoining sewer systems, was approved by Council and carried out in conjunction with the State College Area School District School Board of Education.

The new State College Borough Service Building construction planning was advanced with Council's appointment of a steering committee for the project. In addition, Council appointed a Downtown Master Plan Steering Committee.

Late in 2012, Council passed legislation to notify COG that it intended to withdraw from COG Code Administration starting in January 2014 unless major problems with the organization could be resolved.

2013-2014

During 2013, Council's goals were to tackle problems existing or expected for citizens of the Borough. An ordinance improving the ability of the police to lower the serious problem of noise in the neighborhoods by allowing citations and fines to be increased for problem properties was passed.

The new residential refuse collection system using curbside carts being collected by automated trucks began on April 1, 2013. Organic waste and landfill waste began to be collected in separate containers. This program continues to be successful beyond the original expectations. Monitoring of energy usage was increased. Conservation of amounts of wastewater needing treatment through repairing wastewater lines to prevent infiltration of ground and rainwater into sewage lines was a priority.

Council approved the final plan for the Fraser Centre construction project to move forward. After many discussions, a resolution was passed to not allow the University to build a gas pipeline through the Highlands neighborhood. The gas pipeline from near the Centre Furnace to the University Power Plant on North Burrowes Street was subsequently successfully built with all major construction through campus lands.

The Downtown Master Plan was approved in the summer of 2013. Actions included recommendations beginning immediately and extending over ten years. Plans included marketing, navigating, connecting, living in, and managing the district with goals in each area. Goals of the plan are included in the 249-page final report. Implementation began and continues to date.

The Centre Region Comprehensive Plan was completed in 2013 by COG. The plan included a study of all areas of importance such as land use and housing in the Borough and Centre Region townships, for at least the next ten years.

Several long-lasting projects were completed in 2014. Between 1989 and 2014, individual plans were written for most of the State College neighborhoods. In 2012, it became apparent that a single plan addressing all neighborhoods should be prepared. Themes affecting all neighborhoods as well as concerns of the individual areas, were addressed resulting in a 250-page plan in 2014. The figure on page 4 is a map showing the borderlines of each neighborhood still existing today. Demographics. Unique features of each area, and opportunities for the future are given in this available document.

A Master Plan for Holmes-Foster Park was completed in late 2014. The plan gave core physical improvements, programmatic improvements, and a plan for action over a phased schedule of years as funds became available.

Another large project completed in 2014 was a complete revision and expansion of the Design Guide for properties, including landscaping by the Design Review Board. This useful document contains suggestions for the design of new and redeveloped properties. Safe, attractive, and sustainably built environments were strongly recommended but not required. All suggestions were written to comply with the current zoning and code requirements.

Plans for the redevelopment of a service facility were made. The new facility was sized to serve the Borough for the foreseeable future for the foreseeable future. Frequent flooding was eliminated, and expanded, modern facilities were provided. Further details are included in the facilities section.

Other long-lasting projects for 2014 included plans for revision of the streetscape of the first block of South Pugh Street in 2015, making many intersection improvements downtown to improve safety and aid handicapped persons, and further implementation of the Downtown Plan.

2015-2016

The year 2015 saw the Borough discuss and enact an ordinance supporting an amendment to the commercial district to increase development capacity in the 500 block of East College Avenue. The final ordinance provides an overlay with incentives for including second-floor commercial space, underground parking, professional housing, and LEED certification. Implementation was still in progress in late 2016.

The long-range Holmes Foster Park Master Plan was discussed at length throughout 2015 and approved in late December.

A plan was discussed for the redevelopment of the west side of the 200 block of South Allen Street, where the Borough owns the Verizon Building at 224 S. Allen St. and the parking lot south of the Jeramar Building. The plan would include all properties except the Jeramar Building and the Verizon Building at the corner of South Allen Street and West Foster Avenue. Planning continued into 2016 with approval enacted in November 2016.

A state statute that only the state legislature can pass legislation that would prohibit guns in public buildings (except for police officers) and outside public areas was enacted. The state statute invalidated and mandated the repeal of the Borough's ordinance prohibiting guns in municipal parks. Long discussions ensued opposing this law, allowing guns in municipal public buildings but prohibiting guns in state and county facilities. Council and other Centre Region municipalities objected to no avail.

Additionally, 2015 saw many new apartment buildings being planned and/or constructed. Most of these buildings were in the downtown area, replacing more traditional structures using maximum height and coverage allowed in the commercial district. The large structure at the corner of High Street and East College Avenue (The Rise), the attractive inclusionary housing building at the corner of South Pugh and South Atherton Streets, and several dormitories on North and East campus provide the start to an unprecedented increase in student housing in the community. Also, the initial designs of the massive new State College Area High School on Westerly Parkway show a large community-supported development to be completed over the next four years.

The year 2016 began with Council discussing the inclusionary housing ordinance, parking fund projects, and authorization for borrowing for these projects.

In March, the Department of Neighborhood and Community Services was established to include public health and ordinance enforcement functions; educational programs on food service-related requirements and procedures; and all functions of Community Engagement. Community Engagement sponsors all types of informational programs on regulations and citizen participation opportunities for all portions of the community, including students.

The funding and design of the Dr. Martin Luther King, Jr. Plaza project to be established on the 100 block of South Fraser Street, adjacent to the Fraser Parking garage, was approved by Council.

Suggestions for student home rules to be changed to not include doctoral students in the student category were not passed.

Council strongly supported renovations of, instead of the closures of, Corl Street and Radio Park elementary schools, and replacing them with a school in a different location. The renovation alternative, after much discussion, was later adopted by the School Board in their ongoing facilities review. Such projects were completed in 2019.

Discussions began about building a skate park in the Borough, which was desired by many young people, as there was not one available in the Centre Region. Such discussions continued for several years with a committee appointed by Council making recommendations.

Penalties for marijuana possession were changed from a misdemeanor category to an ordinance violation with a fine as the penalty.

The Design Review Board and Historic Resources Commission were merged as the work of both has many overlaps. The Homestead Investment Program was revised to allow higher costs for buying property, as current limits were no longer viable to allow such acquisitions.

A resolution to favor state legislation against ethnic intimidation was passed unanimously by Council and forwarded to the State of Pennsylvania. A similar resolution on the hate crime commission was later approved.

A Master Tree Plan for the Borough was legislated to provide an urban forestry strategy to effectively manage 'Tree City' and engage in responsive planning in conjunction with the community. The detailed 87-page plan is available on the Borough's website.

2017-2018

The year 2017 saw several important projects of the Borough reach fruition.

After years of discussion of an ordinance establishing a Local Historical and Architectural Review Board to oversee activities in the Holmes-Foster and Highlands neighborhoods, the Board was established. This board requires a review of all proposals to change contributing buildings in these districts. Any proposal to make external renovations, additions, or demolitions must be reviewed. The Board is charged with preserving the key character-defining features of the neighborhoods while still allowing flexibility to property owners.

Five years after Council resolved that the plaza next to Fraser Street Parking Garage would be named the Dr. Martin Luther King, Jr. Plaza, planning began. An advisory committee was formed, and funding was made available to make an open-air facility honoring peace, equality, and justice. The completed plaza was officially opened on Aug. 28, 2017, with a ribbon-cutting ceremony. Usage has been strong since.

Included in 2017 work was the start of a project to comprehensively review and rewrite the Borough zoning ordinances. After many years of adding ordinances, some of which contradicted one another or were unclear, editing and rewriting of zoning ordinances was a major project, with the goal of making the documents more readable and streamlined. This project was a long-term endeavor and has continued for years.

Resolutions and updates of polices on diversity and inclusion were made a priority during 2017. A new committee, the Human Relations Committee, was established to continue the work in these areas.

In 2017, Greenbuild started to build a pair of homes in the 1400 block of University Drive, equipped with green technology to lower energy costs. Borough Council provided the money to buy the land for the State College Community Land Trust. Funds were raised from several other sources to erect the properties. The completed properties provide housing for two income-eligible families to purchase and have been well-received.

At the end of 2017, both the author and the Mayor completed their years of service as elected officials of the Borough. Elizabeth Goreham served 20 years – 12 years on Council and eight years as Mayor, and Thomas Daubert served 24 years as a Council member with three two-year terms as Council President. Both continue to serve in other capacities.

The Borough continued many projects in 2018 to enhance the quality of life and the safety of the residents. Equality issues addressed on many fronts led to the Borough receiving a 98 out of 100 points on the Municipality Quality Index of the Human Rights Foundation. Initiatives of the LGBTQ Advisory Commission are substantially focused on the furtherance of polices on nondiscrimination.

During 2018, the Borough also received platinum certification for its programs to be a sustainable community. Such honor was given to recognize the first municipality-wide food waste collection and composting program on the East Coast, constructing rain gardens to minimize stormwater runoff, and making plans to reduce greenhouse gas emissions, among other programs.

2019

State College created a new strategic plan, which was adopted by Borough Council in 2019, to lead the Borough in future modifications of existing policies and programs, as well as new programs. This long-range plan received much discussion over several years. The plan is available on the Borough's website.

The Town Center Project for the west side of the 200 block of South Allen Street took a step forward with cooperative efforts between the Highland Holding Group and the Borough Redevelopment Authority. The project includes a variety of uses, including a boutique hotel, restaurant, office space, and civic space, and replaces the drive-in bank, the mid-block telephone building, and the parking lot, and adds to the existing building, now containing apartments and a few businesses. Actual plans are being finalized in 2024 and will be followed by construction.

Much work on efforts on housing affordability took place with the Borough working with the State College Community Land Trust and the Temporary Housing Foundation, among other groups, attempting to fill a definite need in the region.

During 2019, police officers were serving a mental health warrant that resulted in the use of deadly force. This incident led to the Centre County Commissioners and the Borough of State College Council appointing the Task Force on Mental Health Crisis Services to evaluate the local mental health system. Discussions around a renewed interest in a community oversight board were also held, along with an interest in establishing a social worker position within the police department.

Several dialogues with the community about diversity and racial equality were held, and work was started in the Borough for a racial equity plan.

2020-2021

Much of 2020 and 2021 was devoted to policies and procedures necessary for dealing with the COVID-19 pandemic. Beginning on March 16, 2020, several measures were approved to enhance physical distancing and cancel events and activities that would result in large gatherings of citizens through June. An ordinance mandating mask wearing and size limitations on gatherings was passed and further modified several times as necessary throughout the remainder of the year.

During the summer of 2020, Council voted to adopt a resolution to be in solidarity with discussions of justice, equity, and action. Discussions of the establishment of a Community Oversight Board continued, leading to the later establishment of the Board. Each of the necessary actions required much discussion throughout the year and, together with standard policies and budget items, required large periods of discussion in the latter part of the year.

Much of the 2021 agenda was a continuation of the 2020 work. The Borough's Race Equity and Leadership project, the Oversight Review Board, and several COVID-19-related items were discussed early in the year.

The Community Oversight Board was appointed, with work beginning in the fall. Progress was reported on the Mental Health Crisis Services report to suggest policies to modify current practices.

Inclusionary housing continued to get much attention to set policies to improve such housing in the Borough. The Borough's sustainability plan was updated.

Several amendments were made to the Temporary Emergency COVID-19 ordinance in order to keep up with changing state requirements, especially on mask usage.

The walkway between Calder Way and East College Avenue, as an extension of McAllister Alley (site of centennial pig statue), was renamed Pat Daugherty Walkway in honor of his long-term service to the Borough and the entire community. Pat was the owner of The Tavern, which abuts the walkway, and passed away on Nov. 7, 2021.

2022-2023

As the nation began to come out of the COVID-19 pandemic in 2022, emphasis on necessary projects and activities, as well as the usual functions, increased. Highlights of the year included the following items.

The addition of the Community Oversight Board and a civilian social worker to the staff of the Police Department began to work to provide guidance on practices to ensure appropriate police policies in relations with the public, as well as internally.

The Diversity, Equity, Inclusion, and Belonging Division began to function with a full-time Director to facilitate all efforts of the Borough in these areas.

Plans for a more connected bicycle network were made to provide State College with an East-West connector to existing bicycle paths in the North-South direction.

The new Mayor of the Borough, Ezra Nanes, took office.

Initial efforts on more forward-looking plans began in 2022.

The year 2023 continued the work of 2022 in all areas, as well as the following highlights.

A sister city relationship with the Ukrainian college town of Nizhyn was established. In May, a memo of understanding to exchange resources on national and cultural matters was approved. The Mayor of Nizhyn visited State College.

State College received a Tree City USA designation for the 38th consecutive year.

Major efforts on the comprehensive zoning rewrite, affordability, and diversity started in 2022, and are continuing from previous years, progressing.

Citizen Recognition Programs
1985-2023

To recognize service over long periods of time, the Borough established the XYZ Awards in 1985 to honor those citizens who served on multiple ABCs with distinction. The Legacy Award was established in 1991 to recognize long-term contributions leading towards community improvement. In 1999, the "Ingrid" award was established to commemorate Dr. Paul Holtzman's late wife, Ingrid P. Holtzman. This award grants $1,000.00 to an individual, organization, or company that has enhanced or contributed to the aesthetic appearance of the Borough. In 2007, the Arnold Addison Award was established to recognize a person or group who has promoted the welfare of the community. In 2020, the COVID-19 Awards were given to those who made efforts to lessen the impact of the pandemic.

These awards credit the many community members and groups who have and continue to improve State College.

XYZ Award

1985	Robert O. Herman	For his work on the Airport Authority and the terminal/facility expansion.
1986	William G. Leitzell	For his work on the University Area Joint Authority (UAJA) and the State College Sewer Authority.
1987	James H. Miller	For his work on the CATA Board.

1991	Harold Zipser	For his work on Council, several ABCs, and on several downtown ad hoc committees.
1992	Richard Barrickman	For his long service on the Parks and Recreation Board/Authority.
1993	James M. Rayback	For his work on the Planning Commission, the Government Study Commission, and the Parking Authority.
1994	Bob Schmalz	For his many years of service on the State College Borough Water Authority.
1995	Jacqueline Melander	For her leadership on the Historic Resources Study Committee.
1996	David Long	For 20 years of service on the State College Borough Water Authority.
1997	Peter B. Everett	For his long and dedicated service on the State College Planning Commission.
1998	Stanford Lembeck	For his long and dedicated service on the State College Zoning Hearing Board.
1999	Jerry R. Wettstone	For his work in promoting parks and open space on the Parks and Recreation Authority.
2000	Dr. Gerald B.M. Stein	For his service on the Parking Authority, Sewer Authority, Commissioner for Pedestrian and Traffic Safety, and Neighborhood Traffic Mitigation Committee.
2001	Bob Ott	For his service in many volunteer positions throughout

Year	Name	Citation
		the County and on the CDBG Citizens' Advisory Committee.
2002	Jeffery Kline	For his leadership throughout the approval process to expand the Schlow Memorial Library.
2003	Mary Ann Haas	For her extraordinary commitment to volunteer service to the Borough.
2004	Rae Chambers	For her work on the Planning Commission and dedication to the well-being of the community.
2005	Emory E. Enscore, Jr.	For his years of service with both the CATA Board and the State College Borough Water Authority.
2006	Edward Buss	For his years of service with the State College Authorities Board, State College Industrial and Commercial Development Authority, and Business Privilege Tax Study Committee.
2007	Christina Rambeau	For her years of service with the Planning Commission, Design Review Board, Transportation Commission, Pedestrian & Traffic Safety Commission, and other ad hoc groups.
2008	Betty Grudin	For her years of service on the CDBG Citizens' Advisory Committee and current service on the Authorities Board.
2009	Rosalie Bloom-Brooks	For her service on the Historic Resources Commission, Urban Village Revitalization Steering

		Committee, and the Zoning Hearing Board.
2010	Anita Genger Eric Boeldt	For their combined and individual service on many ABC's over the past 20 years.
2011	Donna Conway	For her service on several ABC's over the years
2012	William Elmendorf	For his service on the Tree Commission and all of the work he did on the Master Tree Plan.
2013	Mary Barnes	For her service on the University Area Joint Authority, the Transportation Commission, and as an alternate on the Zoning Hearing Board.
2014	Vicki Fong	For her many years of service on the Redevelopment Authority (RDA) and for her efforts in creating economic development workshops.
2015	Marcia Patterson	For her many years of service on the Board of Health and for serving on the CDBG Citizens' Advisory Committee since 2012

Marcia Patterson (left) and Tom Daubert (right) at the 2015 Awards Ceremony.

Photo by the Borough of State College.

2016	Donna Queeney	For her many years of service on the Zoning Hearing Board, Borough's representative t o the Centre R e g i o n a l Planning Commission, and State College Planning Commission member.
2017	James Locker	For his many years of service on the Police Civil Service Commission and for also serving on the Taser Advisory Committee.
2018	Ron Madrid	For his contributions to several committees and commissions.

2019	William Taylor	For his contribution to the Board of Health from 2003 to the present.
2020	Colleen Ritter	For her contributions to the Redevelopment Authority from October 2011 to December 2019.
2021	Larry Miles	For his contributions to the Rental Housing Revocation Appeal Board from January 2007 to the present.
2022	Paul Jovanis	For his contributions to the Transportation Commission from 2003 to 2020
2023	Mark Bergstrom	For his contributions to the CDBG Citizens' Advisory Committee from 1998 to 2008, Civil Service Commission from 2013 to the present, and Community Oversight Board coordinator 2021/2022.

The Legacy Award

1991	Sidney Friedman	For his contributions to the economic vitality and ambiance of the Central Business District of State College.
	Howard W. Higbee	For creating the idea of Sunset Park, organizing the volunteers, and naming the park.
	The Lederer Family	For their donation of the land that became Lederer Park.
1992	Wallis Lloyd	For the founding of the Central Pennsylvania Festival of the Arts.
	Friends of the Library	For their support of Schlow Memorial Library.
1993	Phil Gill	For his many contributions to Little League baseball.
	John Dittmar	For the founding of the public recreation program leading to the Centre Region Parks and Recreation Authority.
1994	Ann Cook	For the founding of the Voluntary Action Center, now Volunteer Center.
1995	Arnold Addison	For 18 years of service to the Borough as a Councilman and Mayor.
	Nittany Valley Symphony	For their many contributions to the musical and cultural lives of the residents of State College and Central Pennsylvania.

1996	State College Women's Club	For 100 years of service to the community.
1997	State College Rotary Club	For service to the community for many years.
1998	Ed Mattil	For his hard work and commitment to the Borough's Centennial Celebration and the creation of the commemorative brick walkway and town sculpture.
	Henry L. Yeagley Jr.	For volunteer Deputy to Mayor Addison from 1978 to 1993.
1999	Alpha Fire Company	For service to the community for many years.
	Henry T. Moon	For service to the community for many years.
2000	Ingrid P. Holtzman	For service to the community for many years.
2001	Euguene W. Lederer	For service to the community for many years.
	International Hospitality Council	For service to the community for many years.
2002	Thelma Price	For service to the community for many years.
2003	The Issues Forum	For service to the community for many years.
2004	Peirce & Felicia Lewis	For service to the community for many years.
2005	Community Alternatives in Criminal Justice	For their commitment and dedication to the well-being of the community, making Community Alternatives in

		Criminal Justice is an agent for positive change.
2006	Housing Transition Temporary Housing	For service to the community for many years.
2007	Marty Starling	For her work with many organizations in the Borough.
	State College Community Land Trust	For their work in providing a much-needed service to low- and moderate-income residents who dreamed of owning a home.
2008	Mimi Barash Coppersmith	For her service to the community through many organizations and the success of the Barash group.
2009	James McClure	For his work with the Borough during the 1960s and 1970s, including his work in the development of the Borough's sign ordinance.
	Centre Life Link	For their many years of service to the community through their ambulance service.
2010	Bill Welch	For his many years of work as a dedicated public servant, community leader, and humanitarian.
2011	Dolores Taricani	For her many years of work, philanthropy, and volunteerism in downtown State College.
2012	Centre County United Way	For their assistance to residents of the Borough, as well as individuals and

Year	Recipient	Citation
		organizations throughout Centre County.
2013	Central Pennsylvania Festival of the Arts	For their efforts and dedication to hosting an event that offers all Borough residents an opportunity to experience art.
2014	State College Food Bank	For their efforts and dedication to providing food to those in need for over 30 years.
2015	Ron Quinn	For his efforts and dedication to providing food, shelter, planning, access to legal, mental health, job resources, and housing to those in need.
2016	Centre County Women's Resource Center	For 41 years of service to the community providing free services and support to women.
2017	Terry J. Williams	For continued service as the Borough Solicitor.
2018	Elizabeth A. Goreham	For outstanding contributions to the quality of community life. Council member for 12 years, President for two years, and Mayor for eight years.
	Foxdale Village	For outstanding contributions to the quality of community life. Foxdale Village was built in 1987 and was completed in 1990.

Elizabeth A. Goreham speaking after accepting the Legacy Award.
Photo courtesy of the Borough of State College.

2019	Thomas Daubert	For outstanding contributions to the quality of community life. An active Council member for 24 years, serving as President three times.
2020	Carmine Presta	For outstanding contributions to the quality of community life.
	Palmer Museum of Art	For outstanding contributions to the quality of community life.
2021	Elaine Meder-Wilgus	For outstanding contributions to the quality of community life.
2022	Charles and Jo Dumas	For outstanding contributions to the quality of community life, including the performance of God's Trombones to benefit the PA Innocence Project.
	Pat Daughterty	For outstanding contributions to the quality of community life. Pat owned the Tavern Restaurant. He

endowed scholarships and served as a director of the Downtown Business Association.

2023   Barbara Farmer   For outstanding contributions to the quality of community life.

            Patricia Best   For outstanding contributions to the quality of community life, which include leading the Mental Health Taskforce.

The "Ingrid" Award

2000	Joel Malnick and Sarah Twibell	For improving the preservation and adaptive reuse of 310 South Burrowes St. and 314 South Burrowes St.
2001	Andrew and Catherine Zangrilli	For doing many things for the betterment of State College.
2002	Joe Banks	For the placement of gardens at various locations in and out of the Borough, using traditional flowers interspersed with vegetable plants.
2003	Michael Pilato	For placing several murals throughout State College.
2004	Fred Fernsler	For his design of many buildings, such as the Alpha Fire Hall and Beaver Gardens, and Borough projects, including the Pugh Street Parking Garage renovation.
2005	Penn State University	For the outstanding design for many projects on campus, including Penn State Downtown Theatre, Eastview Terrance, and Shortlidge Mall.
2006	Graham Curtis	For designing many business signs that add to the rich streetscape downtown.
2007	Schlow Centre Region Library	For the outstanding design of a building that fits the synergy of the downtown.

2008	The State Theatre	For the historic reconstruction of the 70-year-old landmark, which was gutted and rebuilt to provide a venue for theatre, dance, music, and film.
2009	Prime Property Group	For the property located at 700 West College Ave.
2010	The Arboretum at Penn State	For the vision and culmination of The Arboretum project, as an outreach, teaching, and research facility dedicated to preserving beauty and ecological functions.
2011	Community Arts Collective	For their "Dreams Take Flight" mural, located on the McLanahan's building at South Allen Street along Calder Way.
2012	Jeramar Enterprises	For constructing Jeramar Plaza at 226 South Allen St. to fit in well with the downtown streetscape.
2013	David A. Levy & Associates	For the architectural designs created for the Urban Outfitters building, the former M&T Bank site, on East College Avenue.
2014	Phil Hawk	For his skill and craftsmanship as a master stonemason and his work on the newly renovated Nittany Lion Shrine.
2015	Richard and Sally Kalin	For the donation for the "Downtown Eugene Brown" statue in front of the Schlow Memorial Library.
2016	Nicolas and	For improving the appearance of the Borough of

	Carolyn Kello	State College with renovations to their property at 914 Robin Road.
2017	UpStreet Architects, Inc.	For 1311 South Atherton St., for developing an affordable housing project in the Borough that is aesthetically pleasing.
2018	Harper's Shop for Men	For improving the appearance of the Borough of State College.
2019	Penn State's Music Recital Hall	For improving the appearance of the Borough of State College.
2020	Greg and Meghan Hayes	For improving the appearance of the Borough of State College, specifically 915 Robin Road.
2021	No Award Recipient	
2022	Neil & Malgorzata Sullivan	For improving the appearance of the Borough of State College, specifically 315 E. Hamilton Ave.
2023	The Tavern Restaurant	For improving the appearance of the Borough of State College, specifically 220 E. College Ave.

The Arnold Addison Award

2007	Tau Phi Delta Fraternity	For the annual workday in Lederer Park, organized in remembrance of one of their former members and Borough Arborist, the late Jim Evans.
2008	Off-Campus Student Union	For coordinating activities and contributing to the community through philanthropic programs such as Thon and Relay for Life.
2009	Gary Schultz	For his efforts to coordinate and communicate with local municipalities on issues of economic development, emergency planning, and management.
2010	University Park Undergraduate Association	For their many contributions to improving Town/Gown relationships.
2011	Stephen G. Shelow and Thomas R. King	For collaborating on many initiatives and programs, resulting in one of the strongest and most effective partnerships between the university and the downtown police in the country.
2012	Fresh Start	For using their day of service to have volunteers work throughout the Borough on improvement projects.
2013	The Pennsylvania State University Fraternity Council	For noteworthy efforts in 2013 to improve Town/Gown relations, focused on improving communications

		with and oversight of fraternities.
2014	Peg Hambrick	For the Neighbor-to-Neighbor Program
2016	Town&Gown Magazine	For 50 years of publication, it has been informing and entertaining the public.
2017	Lydia P. Abdullah	For work on the Task Force for Policing Communities of Color.
2018	South Hills School of Business & Technology	For outstanding contributions to improving the quality of life and promoting Town/Gown relations in the Borough of State College.
2019	Shoba Wadhia	For outstanding contributions to improving the quality of life and promoting Town/Gown relations in the Borough of State College.
2020	Life Link PSU	For outstanding contributions to improving the quality of life and promoting Town/Gown relations in the Borough of State College.
2021	The Woskob Gallery	For outstanding contributions to improving the quality of life and promoting Town/Gown relations in the Borough of State College
2022	Global Connections	For outstanding contributions to improving the quality of life and promoting Town/Gown relations in the Borough of State College.
2023	Sustainability Institute	For outstanding contributions to improving the quality of

life and promoting
Town/Gown relations in the
Borough of State College.

COVID-19 Awards

2021   The Makery   For making masks during the
                             COVID-19 pandemic, as well as
                             providing masks to Borough
                             employees.

        Centre Volunteers   For their efforts in organizing
        in Medicine   COVID-19 vaccinations and
                             medical care in the
                             community.

The State College Centennial

The college opened its Centennial celebration in late August 1995 and concluded on Aug. 29, 1996. A short record of the events is given at the end of Arnold Addison's book.

The celebration was organized by the Centennial Commission, many volunteers, the elected Council, and Borough staff. Some details, a few pictures, and illustrations related to the celebration and history are recorded here with an emphasis on events and items of lasting interest.

The celebration began with a kick-off dinner on Aug. 26, 1995, for over 100 Borough officials, volunteers, and active residents. The Centre Furnace mansion and grounds was the venue for a short program, dinner, and socialization on a beautiful evening. One of the highlights at the beginning of the evening was the arrival of the Grand Dame of State College, Virginia Dale Ricker, with her friends. At the time, she was in her nineties and arrived driving her vintage convertible. This wonderful event pointed to a very successful year of celebration.

Several projects were undertaken to memorialize the year and remain reminders of the Borough's history.

An iconic photograph taken in 1894 of a pig walking down Easy College Avenue, then a dirt road with a few structures, caused the pig to be chosen as a symbol of the Centennial. A bronze sculpture of three pigs was created by Eric Berg and sits on the McAllister Walkway close to College Avenue. The mother pig was named Centennia for the 100th anniversary of the incorporation of the Borough of State College. The two suckling piglets were named Ed, for education, the cornerstone of the State College community, and Hope, a symbol for the future. The sculptures are permanent residents of the walkway.

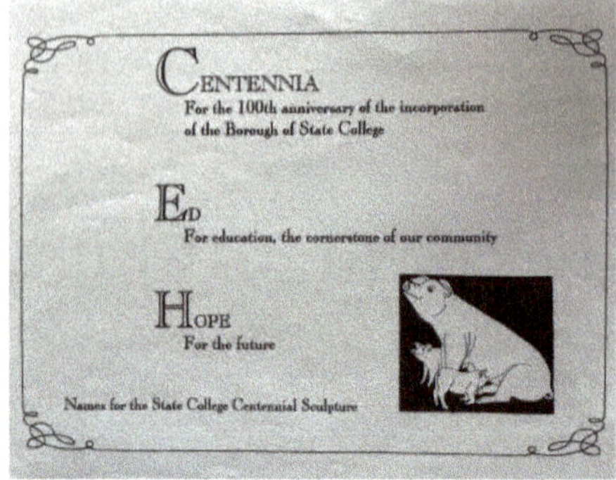

Centennial Pigs and formal names. Photo courtesy of the Borough of State College.

A lasting project for the year was the sale of commemorative bricks installed on the sidewalk in front of the Tavern on East College Avenue and on the McAllister Walkway from East College Avenue to Calder Way. Bricks could commemorate Centennial events or identify organizations or individuals who purchased them. The bricks remain today and provide much visual pleasure when attempting to find specific bricks.

An iron drinking fountain which had been constructed and purchased by a women's community improvement group early in the 20th century, was originally (1907) placed opposite the East College Avenue and Pugh Street intersection in front of the College Avenue walkway. Its purpose was to provide drinking water for citizens as well as a trough for watering horses, livestock, and smaller animals. Later the fountain was moved to the Poschadel home in the 500 block of South Atherton Street. In 1996, Dorothea Poschadel Roberts returned the fountain to the Borough as part of the Centennial, after which it was installed in Central Parklet (now Sidney Friedman Park) on South Fraser Street in August 1996 as part of the celebration. The fountain remains in this location.

A choral symphony titled "Mountain Laurels" was written and produced by Bruce Trinkley, a music professor at Penn State, and was performed for the community with a cast of hundreds at Eisenhower Auditorium as a part of the celebration.

Many artworks were created for the centennial, including a

limited edition print of Holmes Foster Park by Harold Altman; a painting showing ten stained glass and/or steeples of churches in the Borough made into a postcard; a water color of the pig sculpture; and a Centennial quilt made by Centre Pieces Quilt Guild members now hanging in the atrium of the Municipal Building.

State College Centennial commemorative quilt. Photo courtesy of the Borough of State College.

A grand parade was held in early August with many sections, including Borough organizations, bands, and fire companies. The Grand Marshall was Robert Sigworth, a long-time active member and resident of the community, who was approaching his 100th birthday. The parade started on East Campus and proceeded down Shortlidge Road to East College Avenue, moving west to Burrowes Street, and disbanding on campus near Recreation Hall.

Borough Council, Commission members, and other officials rode on an open wagon dressed in summer 1896 attire. Soon after the parade started and reached College Avenue, rain began and continued throughout the procession. Although soaking wet by the end of the parade, the participants and parade watchers continued their enthusiasm throughout.

The celebration was closed by ceremonies in Central Parklet on Aug. 29, 1996, with comments by most of the people who were responsible for the Centennial year events. Memories by longtime residents Edith Virginia Dale Ricker, Vivian Doty

Hench (who earlier wrote 'The History of State College 1896-1946'), Harold Zipser, and Jerry Wettstone were shared with the assembled crowd. Music by the State College Municipal band concluded the observance.

Three books were published as part of the Centennial Celebration. *State College, Pennsylvania, A Photographic Celebration* chronicles a day in the life of State College on Sept. 12, 1994, and was sponsored by the Centennial Commission as one of its first projects, starting at 12:30 am and ending at 11:59 p.m. About 180 people submitted photos for the publication, resulting in 100 pages of multiple photos shown chronologically.

The Story of the Century was written by Jo Chesworth, a Centre Region resident and writer, was published in hardback and contains a liberally illustrated history of the Borough and its activities from many sources.

Issues and Personalities in the First 100 Years of State College Government was written by Mayor Emeritus of State College, Arnold Addison and primarily discusses Borough actions and the elected officials who have served the community until 1996.

These books are available for perusal in the Schlow Centre Region Library.

Time Capsule

As part of the Centennial Celebration, a time capsule was selected to contain historical materials related to the first 100 years of the Borough's life from 1896 to 1996. A public, centrally located space was chosen for the capsule's burial. Central Parklet (now Sidney Freidman Park) on South Fraser Street between Memorial Field and the U.S. Post Office. The capsule site complements the fountain also in the very public space. The capsule was buried at an official ceremony presided over by Mayor Welch, Borough Council, and the Centennial Committee. The capsule is planned to remain buried for 50 years and is expected to be opened by Borough officials in 2046.

A listing of all of the items in the capsule would be very long. The categories of materials are listed below with examples of documents and other items included in each category.

Records of the Borough include a copy of the original Charter of State College; event schedules and programs from the Centennial Celebration; pictures of many types, including a picture of the gathering of as many members of Council as were living and able to attend; as well as the entire history leading to the pig sculpture.

Books included in the capsule include the history of the Borough written by Vivian Doty Hench in 1946, the 50th year of the Borough's charter as a municipality. Copies of the three books written for the Centennial are also buried, including: *The Story of the Century* an excellent history by local writer, Jo Chesworth, *A Photographic Celebration,* which contains hundreds of pictures on one day in the life of the Borough, and *In Service of the Borough,* which details 100 years of government actions and participating officials by Arnold Addison.

Several videos of State College scenes from the past and memories were included.

Items sold to the public during the Celebration — including small copies of the pig sculpture, the Centre Furnace Mansion Museum, and Old Main, as well as written materials, and art such as the 'Early Houses of Worship,' a watercolor print — were also put into the capsule.

Much material on events during the celebration by various organizations, like the Alpha Fire Company, many print and video media groups, cassettes, and CDs, was also included. The trove of material will certainly be interesting to the people in 2046 celebrating the Sesquicentennial of State College.

Facilities
1996-2023
The Municipal Building

Municipal Building 2001 to current. Photo courtesy of the Borough of State College.

The Borough of State College formerly occupied a building in the 200 block of South Fraser Street, which was initially a part of a building owned in the early 1900s by the Alpha Fire Company until 1973, when the company moved to its new building on South Atherton Street. Various modifications were made after 1973 until the size was no longer adequate, and the condition of the building deteriorated with age.

The front of the building, with the plaza to the left (later named by Council as the Mayor Bill Welch Plaza), is shown in the illustration.

In 1990, the Borough began to talk about constructing a new Municipal Building. The site chosen was the current site at 243 S. Allen St., which housed four older buildings between Highland Alley and East Foster Avenue. The Borough acquired these sites for the new Municipal Building.

Initial plans for the replacement of the Schlow Memorial Library as part of the project were bogged down in the Centre Region Council of Governments. Thus, the Borough went its own way in designing a stand-alone building. What was needed was expanded space in every area of government: Police, Public Works, Planning and Zoning, Health, Finance, and Administrative Services. Each area needed to be accommodated.

Council appointed a Municipal Building Advisory Committee in the fall of 1998, consisting of ten citizens with varying ideas and co-chaired by two Council members (McManis and Daubert), to suggest plans for the building to contain both Borough government spaces as well as large amounts of civic spaces for functions and meetings. Council was asked to approve the construction of the current three-story above-ground and full underground stories to serve the Community. The construction of the building began in early 2000, with completion scheduled for late 2001 at a cost estimated slightly above $10,000,000. The building opened in early 2002 with all the facilities needed for the expected functions available.

The Service Building

The Administration Building in Service Area. Photo courtesy of the Borough of State College.

After discussions for about a decade, Borough Council and Staff decided to build a new service facility. The old facility outlived its normal amount of service. The service area is also flooded with any reasonable rainfall. For example, a quarter inch of rain caused the release of 20,000 gallons of water on the site. The existing site just west of South Corl Street was increased in size and reconfigured such that the flooding was mitigated. The facility was completed from 2012 to 2013

The facilities include:

- A large garage area constructed to house the service and maintenance trucks. The heated garage allows refuse, snow plowing, salting, tarring, and other vehicles to operate much more efficiently and easily than was possible when they were stored outside, especially during the winter cold.

- A maintenance garage to allow mechanics to service all Borough vehicles

- A locker room and restroom for employees
- An administrative office building and facilities for all supervisory personnel
- Large open bins under a roof that allow bulk storage of deicing street salt, gravel, and other large volume materials
- A plaza and fueling station for all Borough vehicles
- An outdoor relaxation area
- Convenient parking

Schlow Centre Regional Library

The Schlow Centre Region Library since 2005. Photo courtesy of the Borough of State College.

The Schlow Centre Region Library is located at the southeast corner of East Beaver Avenue and South Allen Street. The original building, which was earlier a U.S. Post Office and was demolished to build the new library in the early 2000s, reopened in 2005. The area of the land used was increased by closing a small part of Highland Alley and the property adjacent to the south, donated by the Borough of State College. The Municipal Building is next to the library on South Allen Street.

The library consists of a parking garage for patrons of the library, which is partially underground with an entrance from a parking lot, which is restricted to library users only.

The first floor of the building consists of: a very large children's area with shelved books and other materials for loan, as well as activity tables for children to use; a large gym-like room for meetings and conferences; the primary checkout and book reservation area; and several workrooms and restrooms.

The second floor of the building is the teenage and adult areas, with many areas of shelved books of regular and large print, audio and video books, and DVDs. In addition, several small meeting or adult activity rooms, as well as staff offices, are located here.

The library has a full program of activities for children and adults.

Dr. Martin Luther King Jr. Plaza

Dr. Martin Luther King, Jr. Plaza.. Photo courtesy of the Borough of State College.

The Dr. Martin Luther King, Jr. Plaza is located in the 100 block of South Fraser Street next to the large parking structure and is used as both a memorial and activity space for Borough events.

The attached excerpt was prepared by Barbara Farmer, who was an influential voice in the construction of the Plaza.

An Excerpt from Barbara Farmer

STATE COLLEGE MARTIN LUTHER KING, JR. PLAZA: A Sanctuary in our Beloved Community

If the Dr. Martin Luther King, Jr. Plaza had a voice, it would ring out loud the impact of its presence in our community! We could hear the expressions of hope, equity, joy, and comfort it has provided for those who use it as a quiet place of peaceful reflection, those who use it as a meeting place, those whole families who see it as a place of confirmation for all people who are worthy of recognition for their contributions in this place as well as in our beloved community.

This public space in State College was purposely renamed on April 16, 2012, by Borough Council under the leadership of Mayor Elizabeth Goreham, after a public hearing. Additionally, Peter Morris, a former State College Borough Councilman, led a motion to rename the Fraser Street Plaza and caused it to be named the Dr. Martin Luther King, Jr. Plaza (the Centre Daily Times Good Life section, Sept. 30, 2018); this generous action has created a life-changing presence in the midst of our community. It speaks to Council's motives to highlight and instill the tenets of Dr. King. Council's voice, through this vote, loudly resounds the hope of fairness, tolerance, uplift, and worthiness of diverse people and cultures. Intentionality, dedication, and commitment are deeply rooted in the creation of this very special brick-and-mortar space.

Since its inception, the programs and activities presented in the Plaza have ranged from designated programs and activities sponsored by the Plaza Committee to honor Dr. King — including his birthday (Jan. 15, 1929), the March on Washington (August 28, 1963), and the date of his assassination (April 4, 1968). The Ribbon Cutting Ceremony celebrated the completion of the Plaza and stands as a memorial to remind citizens of Dr. King's legacy as an advocate for civil rights, a legacy that lives on in the State College community and around the world (taken from the invitation for the Ribbon Cutting Ceremony).

The Plaza also represents a sense of a safe haven for community gatherings on a daily basis, as citizens bask in the calmness and comforting "presence" it offers.

DR. MARTIN LUTHER KING, JR. PLAZA COMMITTEE MEMBERS:

Dr. Barbara W. Farmer, Chairperson

Gary Abdullah

Thomas Brown

Catherine Dauler

Charles Dumas

Carol Eicher

Jonathan Friedman

Elizabeth Goreham, Mayor

Edward Holmes

Kevin Kassab

Lesley Kistner

Dr. Wanda Knight

Dr. Anne Marie Mingo

Douglas Shontz

Carlos Wiley

Other diverse programs have been sponsored by a variety of local organizations (i.e., the NAACP) and community groups to demonstrate their purpose, support, skills, and presence to enhance an atmosphere of togetherness and commonality of community building. It has been a vibrant display of experiences of diversity in action, with unconnected groups supporting each other in enhancing evidence that different is not deficient as we celebrate each other's talents and gifts, while joining hands and hearts together.

Being selected as the first Chairperson of this Committee and working with such a diverse group of people, from the mayors (Bill Welch, Elizabeth Gor- ham, Don Hahn, Ezra Nanes) to Council members whom I have experienced during my stay here in State College in the last 26 years, and the committee's diverse membership, I have come to realize that the "Heartbeat of Hope" working within our beloved community is alive and well.

The Dr. Martin Luther King, Jr. Plaza's presence has increased and enhanced community involvement and provided ways to motivate engagement in community outreach with diverse groups of people who are making a tremendous difference in the lives of our citizens.

Discussions with Borough Leaders

This section is added to record some brief observations by long-term participants in Borough government. The idea was to ask questions of these leaders as to what some of the important actions and programs were, as well as responses to situations of the State College government during their participation. The basic questions are, "What do you believe were some of the most important actions of Council and Staff to benefit Borough citizens and the community?" a n d "What positive improvements and new roles were carried out by the government of State College during your participation?" Obviously, not all questions were answered, and discussions went far away from the questions. The short write-ups that follow are interpretations by the Historian of what items were noted by the participants.

The participants held offices such as Borough Manager, Mayor, Police Chief, or Council Member in the discussions with the Historian and are identified in the following summaries.

Donald Hahn

Served as a member of Borough Council from 1996 to 1999 as one of the youngest members ever elected and again from 2006 to 2013 for a total of three four-year terms. He served as President for his last two years. He was elected Mayor of State College for the 2018 to 2021 term, but resigned after two years to take office as an elected District Judge. He remains, after 30 years of governmental service, as an observant citizen of the Borough and its government.

In our discussions, Don identified quite a few areas where Borough Council and Staff took actions and/or made policies that he reasoned are important to the future of the State College community and the Centre Region. His thoughts both complement and add to the discussion points made by others in these conversations. The author notes below the areas covered with some comments.

Fair Housing Ordinance

In the early 1990s, this somewhat controversial effort was undertaken to make a policy on fair housing to indicate that disregard for human rights could not be used to limit where citizens could be housed. This included sex, race, religion, marital status, sexual orientation, and adult age, among others. Rental housing regulations were later made limiting unrelated persons to three in a unit, as well as the number of such units allowed in neighborhood areas to maintain a residential atmosphere.

Preservation

Building regulations in commercial areas limited the height of buildings to 45 feet except for a few downtown locations where 60 feet was allowed. Dissatisfaction with the 60-foot, Historic Preservation height caused this allowance to be repealed in the last few years in order to preserve the visual image of the Borough and other miscellaneous reasons. Historic Building Ordinance regulations were passed to monitor demolishing or remodeling the facades of historically eligible buildings to preserve State College.

Buildings and Facilities

Discussions of buildings and facilities to serve the community over the long term were constructed during the last 25 years and are all important for the future: The State College Municipal Building in 2001, the Schlow Centre Region Library in 2005, Council of Municipal Government in 2005, the reconstruction of the Welch and Park Forest Pools in mid-2010s, and the State College Municipal Service Building. Such progress is unprecedented.

In addition, The Alpha Fire Company has been made a regional service with new facilities in State College, College Township, and Patton Township. Also, the Centre Area Transportation Authority (CATA) built an expanded facility during this time period. These facilities are indeed allowing the Borough and region to serve the communities far better.

Other than building on the items discussed above, one other item deserves more discussion and some action. Maintenance and improvement of the cooperative efforts with Penn State University, with additional interactions on both a formal and informal basis between Borough staff and elected officials, are needed. In some areas, cooperation is not wanted, but in others, interactions are much too dependent on university upper office holders.

Catherine Dauler

Served as a Council Member from 2000 to 2007 and 2012 to 2018, serving a two-year term as President. Cathy has been active in a number of important projects that have increased the health of State College. She especially considered the following among the best: The Schlow Centre Region Library, discussed earlier, to serve the residents of the Borough and the other members of the Centre Region Council of Governments; the conversion of the State Theatre to public use for performances and films; Borough support of the establishment of the Discovery Space which provides a large number of projects and activities for children in various places in the region; and the very strong support of the Borough for the Skate Park plans by making a portion of the Borough land on Highpoint Park (off Whitehall Road) for the construction — at this writing (late 2024), construction on the skatepark has not yet begun although a large portion of the funds required have been raised.

Also, she believes that Council's establishment of the HARB, requiring approval of building construction in the historic districts, and the earlier establishment of the Downtown State College Improvement District were both important to the Borough's health. Other important items were traffic mitigation and housing legislation.

Thomas King

Started as a police patrol officer in 1981, rising to Sergeant rapidly. He was chosen to be the Chief of Police in 1993, serving with distinction in this position until 2016, when he retired from policing and became the Assistant Borough Manager for Public Safety and Community Engagement. He served for five years in this position and was responsible for working to establish many of the policies and necessary positions in Community Engagement before retiring.

Community challenges requiring Borough cooperation with the University, County, and others were many in the past 25 years and were pointed out in the discussion. New policies were often required as a result of specific incidents. Some of these situations were the Beaver Canyon riots, the Sandusky scandal, the Timothy Piazza death, and alcohol fueled issues during State Patty Days. Responses to events, such as Sept. 11, 2001, and the COVID-19 pandemic, should also be mentioned as events that caused many policies to be made, either temporary or permanent.

Important actions and policies in the Borough begun or modified in his tenure, referred to in our discussions, are noted below:

- Installation of cameras to aid police and provide video recordings in an area of the downtown on East Beaver Avenue and East Calder Way in 2004 and 2005
- Equipping police officers with tasers to be used rather than pistols in appropriate situations was authorized and begun in 2015
- Enhanced cooperative efforts with Penn State police officers were started.

Jesse Barlow

Served as a member of Borough Council from 2016 to 2023 and as its President from 2000 to 2023. The two consecutive two-year terms as President were unusual but reasonable, as we were coming out of the COVID-19 years.

During Council years, several quite important issues were either started or completed that should benefit the Borough government in future years. Those applied to COVID-19 are not discussed here as they ideally will not be necessary in the future.

Jesse noted the following items that will impact the government in the future: The conversion to solar power for operations in the future, revisions of the zoning ordinances to make them understandable for private citizens, businesses, developers, and all citizens of the Centre Region, and lastly, the passing of legislation establishing a specific policy and procedure for interactions.

The return of a twice-a-year meeting between the Mayor, Manager, Council President, and two other Council members with the upper echelons of the University administration, including the President, the Provost, and several Senior Vice Presidents, to discuss mutual areas of concern and necessary policies to benefit both entities was needed and accomplished. The need for more interactions throughout the year is deemed necessary, although access has improved somewhat recently.

Barlow noted that another important action that would most likely improve the governmental policies and regulations would be the consolidation of at least some Centre Region municipalities. Several past efforts have failed, as each municipality seeking consolidation must approve such action by a referendum of the citizens. In addition, municipalities considering consolidation must be contiguous, as Ferguson and College Townships are the only municipalities that meet these criteria. Joint consideration of these efforts should begin again.

Jesse also recommended that planning for the replacement of Borough officials should begin, as several of the upper staff may retire within the next several years. Such an effort should definitely affect policies and procedures.

Ezra Nanes

Elected as Mayor of State College for the 2022 to 2025 term, Ezra has been very active in meeting with many community organizations to both give ideas and receive comments to benefit the Borough in his role as speaker to the community. His comments in our discussions below share his evaluation of the recent actions that will benefit the future of the Borough.

- The creation of the Department of Diversity, Equity, Inclusion, and Belonging with a full-time Director and staff to coordinate the new programs in these areas.

- The designation of State College as a transgender sanctuary city — he noted that citizens are divided on this action, but that most citizens appear to approve of this designation.

- The large multi-year project to materially improve the infrastructure and streetscape of Calder Way from Atherton Street east to at least beyond South Garner Street to make the street a major walkway and bicycle route and a more desirable business address while still serving as a service entrance for properties on College Avenue.

- To join with nine other Central Pennsylvania municipalities in forming a power purchase agreement, which should materially lower power costs.

- To bring the long-term project of the zoning ordinance rewrite to a point near completion, which will be a real improvement to all parts of the community.

- The decision to construct a new parking garage on the land between McAllister Alley and McAllister Street, south of Beaver Avenue, north to Calder Way. The garage will replace the parking in the Pugh Street garage, which is reaching the end of its useful life, and the McAllister deck, and will hold a larger number of vehicles than the current structures.

- The Action Sports Park at Highpoint Park, which will be funded by donations and should be built in 2025.

- Future needs for facilities include the Nittany Arts Center already in major discussions, and a multimodal Transportation Center to consolidate such services.

Ezra also noted the talks on the possible consolidation of municipalities were again recommended to begin, as previously noted in slightly more detail in my talks with former Council President Jesse Barlow. We agreed it may be time.

The need for the Borough to discuss the change to a full-time

Mayor position was also advanced by Mayor Nanes. Such a change would allow work on planning and visions for the future of State College as well as what advantages and disadvantages a consolidated community would bring.

Peter Marshall

Borough Manager from 1986 to 2003 and Council member from 2020 to 2023. (More information in Borough Manager Section.)

In the discussion with Peter Marshal, a large number of important issues and needs were noted where solutions would guide the Borough in the future. The actions taken by Council and Staff since 1996 to address many of these areas are listed below.

- Acquired property for the site of the new Municipal Building previously described to make the Borough government work more efficiently and effectively as the community changes and grows.

- Designed and constructed the new system, which was previously designed to make all public services of the Borough run more smoothly.

- Added a large parcel of land to Orchard Park, which was designed and constructed by a sizable Pennsylvania grant, and provided fields and other recreation facilities.

- Regionalized the fire service, adding to Alpha's resources.

- Acquired a large, partly forested area east of University Drive and south of Easterly Parkway and Walnut Spring Lane, which was then partially developed as a walking and picnicking area, and named it Lederer Park in honor of the previous owner of some of the land and a lifetime Borough philanthropic citizen.

- Purchased a parcel of land across University Drive from Lederer Park to be maintained mainly forested with no construction as a National Park Area.

Other items of importance carried out during the Marshall managership, which were new and continue to be important to the Borough are listed below.

- Downtown camera, as discussed under Thomas King.
- A police training program, including professionalism, is still in operation today.
- Ordinances designed to reduce disruption in the neighborhoods, including a point system that has been used to make decisions on what properties display behaviors against Borough ordinances, could retain rental ordinance licenses.
- An ordinance defining the number of rental housing units to non-families that could be licensed in sections of neighborhoods as specified in the ordinance
- Began beautification of areas along major street rights-of-way.
- State College Community Land Trust to offer affordable owner-occupied homes.
- Closed the north end of North Allen Street to manage cut-through traffic in College Heights.

The large number of actions noted is representative of the late 1990s and early 2000s, the Borough has taken to improve the lives of the citizens of State College and the Centre Region.

Thomas Fountaine, II

Borough Manager since November 2003. (More information in Borough Manager Section.)

In discussions with Tom Fountaine in preparing this publication, many programs and issues important to the future of the Borough were noted. Some of the new efforts that do not include everyday normal business are recorded here. The large volume of work during the COVID-19 pandemic is not discussed, as it hopefully will not repeat itself in the future.

A large amount of effort was made in writing policies and procedures to make the community safer and more welcoming to all, whether individuals are short-term visitors or Borough residents. Community Diversity Policing was a major result of this. Affordable Housing now receives a higher priority. The Community Engagement Office was staffed to support and initiate additional policies.

The Borough staff and elected officials were instrumental in making agreements so that Fraser Centre could be developed in the 100 block of South Fraser Street. The building contains retail stores, an attractive hotel, and high-quality condos.

A large Borough government effort is underway to complete a rebuilding of much of the east side of the 200 block of South Allen Street, which is called "Towne Centre." The new construction is not residential and is expected to contain a hotel with two restaurants as well as commercial spaces.

A complete study of the Borough zoning ordinances, some of which are many years old, has been undertaken over the past several years. It is currently nearing its conclusion and will be very helpful in eliminating inconsistencies in the previously amended current codes.

Calder Way improvement began with the replacement of most underground utilities. This also includes reconstructing the street and adding to the streetscape. Some redevelopments should follow.

These projects and changes are only some of the larger happenings so far under Tom's leadership to date.

More Information

For more information, you can go to the Borough's website at https://www.statecollegepa.us.

As of 2024, you can access Council's meeting agendas and minutes, find further information on the Authorities, Boards, and Commissions, and information on the Borough's various governmental departments on the Borough's website. Budget information, Borough codes, and ordinances are posted for the public. The Borough's services and facilities are listed as well. Some studies carried out over the past 10 to 15 years are also available from the website. Some examples are shown below.

Design Guide for the Borough of State College (streetscapes and sustainable sites) 120 pages

State College Neighborhood Plan (recommendations for each of the Borough neighborhoods) 250+ pages

Master Tree Plan for State College Borough 87 pages

State College Downtown Master Plan (general plan and specific attachments)

The Centre Region Comprehensive Plan, 122 pages and attachments

Other regional plans and reports of the Centre Region Council of Governments (COG) are available on the COG website: www.crcog.net

Specific items listed above are as of November 2024 and are subject to change.